WRITING THE HAWAI'I MEMOIR

Advice and Exercises to Help You Tell Your Story

BOOKS BY DARIEN GEE

FICTION
An Avalon Christmas
The Avalon Ladies Scrapbooking Society
Friendship Bread

NONFICTION
Writing the Hawai'i Memoir

ANTHOLOGIES
Don't Look Back: Hawaiian Myths Made New
(contributor)

WRITTEN AS MIA KING
Table Manners
Sweet Life
Good Things

WRITING THE HAWAI'I MEMOIR

Advice and Exercises to
Help You Tell Your Story

BY *Darien Gee*

WATERMARK
PUBLISHING

ISBN 978-1-935690-53-5

Library of Congress Control Number: 2014935551

Design, illustrations and production
Mae Ariola

Watermark Publishing
1000 Bishop St., Suite 806
Honolulu, HI 96813
www.bookshawaii.net
info@bookshawaii.net

Printed in the United States

*Dedicated to **Stephanie Bengene
Lindsey** who called me her own from the
first day we met and showed me
what it means "to be Hawai'i"*

TABLE OF CONTENTS

PULE HOʻOMAIKAʻI

Dedicated to this book, *Writing the Hawaiʻi Memoir*, and those who read it

BY DANNY AKAKA JR.

E ko mākou Makua i loko o ka Lani a me ke Keiki a me ka ʻUhane Hemolele. E nā ʻAumākua, e nā Kini akua, e nā Kūpuna a pau...

We offer this humble prayer of thanksgiving for all of the gifts that have been bestowed upon us, for our senses of *ʻike* (sight), *hoʻolohe* (hearing), *hanu* (smell), *hoʻopā* (touch) and *hoʻāʻo ʻai* (taste), that we may enjoy the beauty and bounty of your Creations and all that Nature has to offer.

We are grateful for the *Hā*, the Breath of Life, the life force and essence that we share with others who are willing to accept the Spirit of Aloha. We offer this with all humility. We are grateful for the profound experiences life has to offer. We happily share this with others through our stories.

We *mahalo* our *kūpuna* who have passed down their precious heirlooms, in the way of *moʻolelo* of their past, so that we may be educated and enriched by the values and lessons of life that these stories have to offer.

We ask for guidance and inspiration that we may continue to share the memoirs of our lives and that we in turn may inspire others to truly follow in this path of enlightenment. And as we now close our earnest prayer, may our words become the string of pearls, a cherished *lei* made with love and care, which we bestow upon others to enjoy.

ʻĀmama, ua noa, lele ka pule, lele wale aku la.

Our prayer is complete. It is free. Let it fly and be accepted in the Heavens.

Daniel Kahikina Akaka Jr. is the director of cultural affairs at the Mauna Lani Resort on the island of Hawaiʻi. He hosts the "Twilight at Kalāhuipuaʻa" program, which perpetuates Hawaiian folk storytelling ("talk story") through music and hula. His uncle, the late Rev. Abraham Akaka, Kahu of Kawaiahaʻo Church, named Hawaiʻi the "Aloha State." Danny follows his uncle's legacy of perpetuating the culture, essence and spirit of Hawaiʻi.

FOREWORD

BY PAMELA YOUNG

My grandfather's portrait hung in the living room over the piano for many years. He died when I was one, so I remember nothing of him. I was always afraid of that portrait, with its cold eyes and thin lips. He looked mean. And no one dispelled that image because no one ever spoke of him.

Decades later, after my father's death, we found a document in a safety deposit box. It was my grandfather's petition to the U.S. Immigration Service to let his Chinese bride into the country, to join him in his new life in Hawai'i. The picture of the man stapled to the document bore little resemblance to the face in the portrait. Something happened to him in the years between. Somewhere the hope and eagerness in his young eyes were replaced by fatigue and a chilling deadness. What happened?

I will never know because Gung Gung (Grandfather) Young was not to be mentioned. That's the way it was back then. Families were so focused on the future they often refused to look back, especially on the darker side of personal history. And so my sisters and I lost a vital part of our immigrant past, an important insight into what made our parents the way they were, and subsequently, what made us the way we are.

That is why we now must speak, must write, must remember.

Recently I had the privilege of writing someone else's memoir, *My Name is Makia,* with the inspiring Makia Malo, a Kalaupapa Hansen's disease (leprosy) patient. Due to the effects of Hansen's, he was unable to chronicle his own story, and so I was entrusted with his memories. At first, we listed his fondest remembrances, accomplishments and triumphs. As time went by he felt comfortable enough to share the more painful memories, the times he acted cruelly and irresponsibly, the lapses in judgment that today cause him deep shame. And after a while, a full life began to take shape on paper.

Writing a life story is like creating a quilt. You look at each piece, print and texture. You begin to see a pattern, then another. And then the patterns begin to intersect with one another and eventually you are able to sew a vibrant, cohesive patchwork.

Dealing with memories is like that. You don't know where the scraps come from. The colors may clash, the fabric may be frayed, but somehow it will all make sense to your descendants and, more importantly, to you. The process alone will change and validate you.

It matters not if your memoir ever makes it to the bookshelves or e-reader digital stores. Publication may not be your goal. It doesn't matter if the memories are incomplete. Had my grandmother learned to write, she might have recorded her feelings when she finally left her homeland or at the births of each of her ten children. Any small detail of her life would have been treasured. Knowing her hopes and fears would have lent so many colors to the palette with which I paint her memory. This is the true inheritance I wish I had received, the words that would have answered my questions about the man in the portrait and the woman he sent for.

I do a lot of writing on airplanes. I put the words down on a yellow pad. I use a pen because I find the scratching of a pencil distracting. I don't correct grammar or spelling. My penmanship sucks. I just scribble whatever comes to mind. Some of it will end up in a story on the five o'clock news, but most of it will stay on that yellow pad and be seen by no one else. Ever.

It's not important if you use a pen or laptop or quill. It's not important if you're on a plane, at your desk or on the toilet. You just have to write down those thoughts and feelings as they emerge. If it's easier to say the words out loud, say them into a recorder.

In this book, *Writing the Hawai'i Memoir*, Darien Gee will guide you on what to do with those words, how to craft and mold them into a memoir. But the first step is all you. Speak, write, remember.

Pamela Young is a broadcast journalist with KITV (ABC) Honolulu, co-author of My Name is Makia: A Memoir *(Watermark Publishing, 2013) and a contributor to* Mid-Week, Off Camera *magazine and several travel and culinary periodicals. She is the recipient of a Peabody and eleven Emmy Awards from the NorCal Academy of Television Arts and Sciences.*

HOW TO USE THIS BOOK

This book was written to help you tell the stories of your life. It can also be used for family history projects, biographies, school projects, personal essays or journal entries. It's my hope that this book will be many things to many people, and that you'll be inspired to find your own way to use it.

YOU ARE HERE

Begin at the beginning. You can jump in anywhere, of course, but if this is your first time picking up the book, I recommend reading it straight through first. Orient yourself, see what you've got, let yourself zero in on the areas that will be most helpful. Let the book guide you through the process, doing the work so you don't have to. This book is your scout, chopping through vines and pushing aside wayward branches so you can stay on the path of writing your memoir.

THE EXPERTS

No man or woman is an island, even if you live on one. While writing this book I came across local authors, academicians, journalists, professors, everyday writers and *kāhuna* who generously offered their own words of wisdom about writing life stories. You'll find their voices in these pages as well.

HO'Ā'O: TRY THIS

What would a writing book be without writing prompts or exercises? You'll find them at the end of each chapter and scattered throughout the book. Use them to help jump start a thought or to kick off your writing. Writers tend to spend a lot of time in their head, so this book will help make sure you're taking the time to get it all down on paper, too.

HŌʻIKE HOʻOPŌKOLE: CHAPTER SUMMARIES

At the end of every section is a chapter summary that recaps key ideas and thoughts. It's a fast way to get you back on track or to give yourself a gentle reminder or confidence boost. I've collected the best of these thoughts and made them into flash cards if you'd like to keep them handy. Visit legacyislepublishing. net for more information.

THE APPENDICES

The back of the book contains several appendices full of additional information on writing other forms of life stories along with additional resources.

HAVE FUN

Finally, have fun. Approach this work with courage, curiosity and hope but let it be something you enjoy. Life is too short not to find happiness in the things we do, and writing your memoir is no exception. Don't pressure yourself to write—consider it more of an invitation.

Komo i ka hana. Let us begin.

INTRODUCTION
WHY TELLING YOUR STORY MATTERS

Sharing Your Mana'o

There are many reasons to tell the stories of your life, and probably just as many reasons not to. *Who would read it? What would other people say? And perhaps the biggest question of all, How or where do I begin?*

Telling the story of your life is not an easy task. (If we're going to do this work, we're going to be honest, right?) But just because it's not easy doesn't mean that it's necessarily hard or that you shouldn't do it at all. Sometimes focus, clarity and a sense of purpose can be enough to get us started.

See yourself standing on a beach, gazing out at the great body of the Pacific. The ocean represents possibilities—boundless, abundant, never ending. So much exists in the water that we cannot see—beauty, mystery, dangers. We can stand on the shore and contemplate, or we can get in and experience it for ourselves. Be courageous. Take a step in.

Let the water lap around your ankles, then wade in to your knees. You start remembering. *My father never talked about what happened during the war* or *Oh, right, Fukushima's used to be there before Long's took over.* You write that down, even though you're not sure where it's going. You walk in a little more, going deeper, and let your feet leave the sandy bottom. Tread water for a little while.

What else? *I remember the taste of gummy candies dusted in* li hing mui*, how sticky the back of my neck felt at dinner time, my first kiss.* Now you're swimming.

As the memories come, you keep writing. And writing. After a while, you may grow tired. It may seem like you've gone as far as you can go, that maybe you don't have anything left. You try a new stroke, something different—you play with dialogue, point of view, details, sift through old letters and newspapers and photographs. You sit down and interview someone from your past. You discover something new or long forgotten, and write, write, write. You take each new thread, each possibility, each secret, and follow it. When you look up, you see you're still swimming, that you've managed to not only stay afloat but have made some progress (Even if the last few strokes have been doggy paddle. That counts, too).

What next? You float on your back, take inventory. You've made some impressive distance, perhaps more than you'd intended, maybe less, and it's time to turn around, time to head back to shore. Relief! You're more than halfway there, the rest should be easy, right?

Except you're tired. Doubt sets in. You worry about how you look, all wet and soggy and amateurish. Maybe you should push yourself forward a little more before turning back. You think about someone who's gone farther than you, those really good swimmers, like your cousin Pono. You wonder if your strokes are any good. Maybe you were too ambitious. Why swim (why write)? It would have been so much easier to just lay on the beach, right where you started. After all, that's where you'll end up.

Fear sets in. What are you doing? Whose idea was it to take this swim in the first place? You remember a recent shark attack. Another beach, another island, but still. Your uncle has always told you not to swim these waters and to spend your time doing something else (like getting a real job) and yet, here you are, doing it anyway. He's going to be mad, boy, oh boy. He'll probably talk stink about you when you get back, about how you never listen, about how the only person you care about is you (So selfish!). You can see his face, angry and red. You don't think you can make it. You might just drown, here and now.

But then, guess what? A turtle swims by. And then another. They're followed by a swimmer, someone in much better shape than you, someone who does this all the time by the look of it. She offers you a smile, a thumbs up. "Flip on your back!" she tells you. "You're almost there." You watch her swim on, her strokes long and confident and strong, and think, *Okay, maybe I can go on a little more.* You keep writing, doubtful but encouraged. You don't give up.

The beach, which once seemed so far away, looms up close now. You feel a surge of energy and adjust your strokes again, more efficient, more purposeful. You recognize the rocks that frame the cove of the beach. You're close. You could walk the rest of the way in if you had to. Knowing that seems to be enough, and you swim forward a few more feet.

You did it. You did it! You see the other swimmer on the beach, the one you met in the water, toweling off. She grins, gives you a shaka. "Way to go!" she calls out.

Every leg of this metaphorical swim is not unlike what you might experience when writing your book, be it a memoir or biography or family history. You'll draw on your many resources, you'll have help, you'll have doubt, you'll hear critical voices or even be dissuaded from pushing on. You'll have moments of rest, moments of clarity, moments of inspiration and pure joy. All the while your pages keep adding up, one after another. Because that's how it begins, pen to paper, fingers to the keyboard, your voice to a recorder.

So come on. Jump in. This is Hawai'i, after all, and water not only surrounds us, it sustains us. It moves through the 'aina—this land, this place we call home. From the clouds to the mountains, to the waterfalls to the streams, all water finds its way to the ocean. The water's warm, and it beckons. No more waiting—let's go.

YOUR MANA'O—YOUR EXPERIENCE IS LIKE NO OTHER

In Hawaiian, *mana'o* means several things—thought, belief, intention, ideas, desire. Your mana'o emanates from who you are as a person. It is individual and unique.

Ho'o is a causative prefix. When you add it to the beginning of a word, it changes the word to one of action—it causes someone or something to do or be something. Is it any surprise, then, that *ho'omana'o* means to remember? Remembering is how your book will get written. You don't need anything else.

No one can write the book that you are going to write. It's as simple as that. Even if you are not writing about yourself, but of someone close to you or within your community, even an icon or historical figure, what you ultimately end up writing about, and *how* you end up writing about it, is your decision. You'll arrive at this decision—and many others—based on your beliefs, perceptions, experiences and personal desires.

> *"We are all creatures of our experiences."*
> **BEN CAYETANO**

You get to claim your life, your experiences, your story. What you put down on the page is up to you. You are the only one who can put the words down in that way.

WHY THIS WORK IS IMPORTANT

Sharing our lives opens us up. It connects us. It helps us (as the writer) to make sense of things, to celebrate moments that might otherwise be lost, to remember what matters most. It helps us (as the reader) to see that we're not alone, that our lives are both personal and universal, that the human spirit is deeper and more profound than we may remember when we're trying to pay our bills or care for a sick child or parent. We get to be a part of another person's experience. We can share the joys, the laughter, the chicken skin coincidences, the sorrow, the grief. We can take what we learn and apply it to our own lives. Then we can turn it around and do the same for others.

> *"So who should tell their stories of Hawai'i? The answer, and not theoretically, is anyone."*
> **CRAIG HOWES**

There are other reasons, too, all good and wonderful and important in their own way. Wanting to capture the story of *tūtū* or *tūtū kane* before they pass or can no longer remember the details of their lives, learning and sharing life-changing events that affected both individuals and a community at large, such as Kapoho (a Big Island town overrun by lava during the 1960 Kīlauea eruption), Kalaupapa (which served as a leprosy settlement from 1873-1969), tsunamis (1946, 1952, 1957, 1960, 1964, 1975) or Pearl Harbor (1941). Other reasons may include preservation of cultural icons, from surfers to *paniolo* to businessmen and businesswomen, politicians or musicians. Wisdom from *kāhuna*, of those who hold Hawai'i in their bodies, minds and spirits. All of these stories are important, and all have their place in history and in our lives. Getting these stories down on paper is one way to ensure that those who come after us will remember, too.

WHAT MAKES US HUMAN

> *"The Hawaiian word for stories, mo'olelo, is a common term for all the life stories that connect us, whether through myths, legends, folktales, parables, histories, biographies, fairytales or oral traditions."*
> **BOB BUSS**

The stories of our lives make us human. It goes beyond the everyday motions of getting up, brushing your teeth, having breakfast, going to school or work, looking after your children, grandchildren, parents. What makes us human and different from other animal species is our ability to feel. Our emotions. Our use of language. Our creativity. We can look at an experience and understand it, dissect it if we choose. Other species have some or all of these attributes as well, but a human being has the capacity—the ability and the will—to do what he wants with it. Anything is possible. The sky is the limit.

THE CALL TO WRITE

So why write? Why not get someone else to write your story for you? Your neighbor Lani used to be an English teacher—she's much better with this writing stuff. Your grammar is terrible, you have lousy handwriting, you don't know how to use a computer. You don't even *have* a computer. You don't have time. This writing stuff is hard, you were never very good with it. You have a great story, yes, many great stories in fact. Oh, what a book this will make! You just need to find someone else to write it all down.

Have you got a mirror handy? Hold it up and gaze into it. Look at that person, at the color and shape of their eyes, their nose (From Mom? Dad? Broken in a wrestling match or car accident?), their mouth (Who was the last person to kiss those lips?). Look at the hairline, the hair (Wavy? Straight? Sun bleached? Roots growing in? None at all?). The neck, the creases. That person, with the bushy or well-plucked brows, the moles, the dimples, the pimples. That person is the best person to write this book. Of that I can promise you.

> *"Keep writing and you will know. In time your writing will speak back to you."*
> **FRANCES KAKUGAWA**

It's not to say that you can't get help. Help is good and help can sometimes make all the difference. But your story will ring clear and true if it starts from you, from your heart and body. You'll know what the tangents mean, the side stories, the way a memory feels. You'll know what's important, what's not. Someone may think that the day you graduated high school was important, but maybe it wasn't, not to you. Maybe it was the day you bumped into a stranger, a tourist, a hitchhiker, an old friend and something happened that only you know about, but it changed your life forever. Why? That is the question and only you have the answer.

The page you are looking at now was, at one time, completely blank. It would have remained blank had a first thought not come into my mind. And then I, through a series of decisions and my own personal preferences and desires, chose the first word to write. Another followed. And so on and so on.

It'll be the same for you. Your job is to bring your story to the page and share it the best way you know how.

But that's not all. Entering into this work by knowing you have a story is only one part of the equation. The other part is understanding what you want to do with it. In other words, what are your intentions? Determining the importance (to you) of actually finishing the work sets another parameter on your path. Are you just exploring and seeing where it goes, or do you expect to write and complete a book-length work? Are you wanting to ensure that your children and grandchildren know about your life or do you hope to publish it to a larger audience?

Is writing this book important to you? Maybe it's not. Maybe it seemed like a good idea, or your mother insisted that you write down the family story (or her story) because you are such a good writer. Maybe you have a story to tell, something you've kept inside that's itching to get out. Maybe you're getting paid to write your book. Maybe you want to tell your life story to future generations you won't have a chance to meet. Maybe you think it'll be fun. Maybe you've lived a rich and varied life and people are always telling you to write your memoirs. Maybe you've always dreamed of writing a book. These are all good and valid reasons—not one of them is wrong or any less noble. *You* just need to know why you're writing this book.

Why? Because there will be times where you will want to give up. Where this good idea suddenly seems like a terrible idea. But knowing why you're writing this book will see you through the challenges and roadblocks. It will help you finish.

HO'Ā'O: TRY THIS

Start with Why

Consider the following four questions and write your responses in a journal or notebook. The more succinct your answers, the better. Having clear, simple intentions makes them easier to remember:

1. Why am I writing my memoir?
2. Why now?
3. How would I feel if I didn't write my memoir?
4. How will I feel when I finish writing my memoir?

BUT I'M NOT A WRITER

If you know how to write, you are a writer. It's as simple as that. You may be a terrible speller, suffer at the thought of writing a single paragraph or hate reading anything over two pages, but you are a writer.

And you already possess all the material you need—your memories. While you may want to look for ways to develop and improve your basic skills (such as punctuation, grammar, story structure), the first thing you must work on is your own thoughts, especially the negative ones. This trumps everything else, because tormented, unhappy writers are no fun at all. Don't sabotage yourself or your abilities. Don't cut yourself off before you've even begun. You need to be your own number one supporter, your own sidekick, your own muse, your own therapist.

> *"The best piece of advice about writing that I ever got was from my uncle, John Kneubuhl. He simply said, 'Find your voice, and honor it.'"*
> **VICTORIA KNEUBUHL**

As with any art, you need to cultivate a respect for the craft. You need to find the parts that you love. And you need to appreciate and celebrate your own gifts and abilities that are going to support you in writing your memoir.

We've all read wonderful and terrible books, seen wonderful and terrible movies. You know that even blockbusters have their critics, too. In short, it's impossible to please everyone, so don't even try. This writing path is about you and writing your truth. Let everyone else write their own memoirs.

Don't put yourself down. Be kind. Trust your words. Trust your desire to write. I know you can do it—shouldn't you, too?

CHAPTER ONE
GETTING STARTED

Hoʻomaka

For some people, beginnings are like a breath of fresh air. A clean white sheet, a mind full of ideas and possibilities. Your pencils are sharpened or your laptop is powered up, the cursor blinking with expectation. You got a good night's sleep, you've had your coffee and you're ready.

For others, beginnings are absolutely terrifying. That same white sheet—how will you ever fill it? Where do you begin? You don't really have a nice, quiet place where you can write—maybe after you clean up that extra bedroom or corner of the living room, then you can begin. A plant would be nice. You're always reading about how important plants are. Maybe you should take a quick trip to Ace Hardware or the local nursery, and see what they have. You suddenly remember a few other things you should do first. You forgot to call Aunty Kealoha yesterday, and you need to take your garbage to the dump. Once those tasks are out of the way, then you can begin, right?

No matter what you're feeling, I have some good news for you. Writing doesn't care if you're dressed in a suit or writing in your pajamas. It doesn't care if you're using index cards or sticky notes or writing on the back of a cocktail napkin. If you're sitting at the library, or in an office, or at the beach, or at the kitchen table, writing is fine with all of that.

START WHEREVER YOU ARE

Writing is ready when you are, wherever you are. All you need are the thoughts in your head, something to capture them—pen and paper, typewriter, computer, voice recorder, whatever suits you best—and a place to sit still and just do it. If your house has too many distractions, hit a coffee shop or a restaurant. Perhaps you need the stimulation of outdoor breezes in a park or at the beach. I've written whole chapters in my car, waiting for my kids. It's not ideal, but it's possible, and looking for creative solutions to life's everyday challenges will help you finish this book.

> *"Close the door, sit down and start. Remember that all writing starts with a draft, and the draft doesn't have to be good, it just has to exist."*
> **LESLIE LANG**

SETTING GOALS

Never ending to do list? No problem. Phone ringing off the hook? They'll call back. Establishing a schedule or routine is essential when it comes to writing, because life has a way of getting in the way. There are numerous demands that seem more pressing and when you sit down to start writing, they'll call to you even louder.

The key is to start simple. There's nothing wrong with setting an ambitious goal, but you want to set yourself up for success. That means having a clear idea of what you want to achieve and establishing a rhythm that works with the realities of your life. Twenty minutes or three pages a day may not sound like much, but you'll know when you're ready for more.

> *"If you want to be a writer, you have to write every single day without fail. This does not mean all day or even most of the day. It only means every day, at least for an hour or so, even when you're busy with work or school or raising your kids or all three."*
> **MARK PANEK**

Better to start at a place that feels easy than one that feels too hard.

You're not a writer if you're not writing (and there's its corollary—if you're writing, you are a writer). So set it up so that you're writing every day, even if it's just a little bit. Turn off the phone, set the timer, get your butt in the chair and don't move until you're done.

Even if you're not exactly sure which direction your writing project is going, warming up your writing muscles is a good idea. Daily practice can make all the difference in the world. So even if you're not ready to start writing your memoir, you can begin to write anyway. This book contains lots of prompts and ideas to help get you started, and some may even develop into a story you'll include in your book. Many writers say that you can't really understand what your story is about until you start writing.

HOʻĀʻO: TRY THIS

Make a Plan

First, choose a start date. Even if you don't know exactly what you'll be writing about, look at the calendar and choose a date within the next week to begin (Yes, we are starting now!):

My start date: _____

Next, choose one measure to govern your writing time:

* Length of time (ten minutes, half an hour, three hours)

* Word count (most computer programs have a way of tracking or telling you your word count—as a rule of thumb, one page that's double-spaced with one-inch margins using Times New Roman font, 12 point, equals approximately 250 words)

* Page length (Two pages? Three pages? Ten?)

I will write _____ (length of time, word count or page length) each time I sit down to write.

ESTABLISHING A ROUTINE

Self-discipline is a challenge for writers, especially new ones. There's an assumption that you either have self-discipline or you don't, but it's actually a skill that you can develop with practice. You'll need it when you're writing your memoir, and fortunately there's a short cut—establishing a writing routine.

Many people approach writing a book in a haphazard way. They sit down, write a few words, organize their desk, get up for a cup of coffee, write some more, take a bathroom break, check their email, do some laundry, make a sandwich, then throw in the towel for the rest of the day because it's time to pick up the kids or catch the evening news. There's nothing wrong with this, but if you want to write a book—more importantly, if you want to *finish* writing a book—you greatly increase your chances by establishing a routine.

Routines are about how we do something. You have a goal in mind, such as keeping the house clean or getting to school or your job on time. Routines ensure that you meet your goal—they're the framework that helps hold everything up so you can do what you set out to do.

Athletes use routines before a game. These routines are sometimes referred to as pre-game rituals, and are designed to get the athlete in the right frame of mind to play (and win). Sometimes these routines are obvious, like an intense warm-up or stretch. Other times they're a bit wacky or off the wall, like touching their nose before they pick up a baseball bat or eating nothing but shrimp for two days before the big game. These routines and rituals tell your mind and body that it's time to get serious. Game on. It's the same with you.

> *"Though I have friends for whom a writing schedule is very important and dear, I came up in newsrooms where you have to produce stuff on a deadline no matter what. I haven't had much control over my schedule. Like most reporters, I can write anywhere, anyplace, anytime regardless of distractions. It's not a talent. It's survival."*
> **LEE CATALUNA**

Not everyone needs a routine to write, but if you want to write and find that you're having trouble doing so, consider adopting a simple routine that will help make writing a regular part of your schedule. Once you know *when* you're going to write, decide *how* you're going to write.

Here are some simple routines that can help train your brain to get ready to work:

* Clear your desk or kitchen table, even if it means putting everything on the floor temporarily except for your computer or notebook.
* Go for a walk.
* Set the kitchen timer for the length of time you will be working.
* Turn off your cell or home phone.
* Shut down your email.
* Make a pot of coffee or have a carafe of water and a glass nearby.

It's important to link these routines together. For example, clear your desk and ready it for work, then go for a ten-minute walk. When you come home, set your kitchen timer and go straight to your desk and begin writing.

Routines won't make you into a writer. But having a routine will establish a pattern or rhythm that can help you get the work done. Routines bring an awareness to every action, and that awareness will carry over into your work.

FINISH WHAT YOU START

Consider setting a completion goal date for your memoir. Seem premature? It's not. Do you want to write your memoir, or do you want to write and finish your memoir? It may seem like an odd question, but there are lots of writers who write without ever finishing their manuscript. If they finish, great; if they don't, no biggie. Others may hope to have a book contract and need a polished, completed manuscript in order to get a publisher. Some may want to have a finished copy so a friend or family member can read it before they pass.

> *"Always start like you mean to finish."*
> **PHIL SLOTT**

Setting a deadline isn't meant to quash your creative spirit. It provides focus, and when the brain puts its full attention on something, it filters out everything else. This happens whether you're aware of it or not. Watching TV is a great example of this—you can shout, yell, do a little dance but short of turning it off it's almost impossible to get someone's attention once they're engrossed in a good show or movie.

Here's the other thing: you can always change your mind. You can move the deadline up or push it back, but you must set a deadline when you begin. Without it your writing project will be unmoored, left to float about and be pushed around by circumstance or whimsy. The brain loves parameters, and it will rally all your resources around it. So whether you're a left-brainer (more of a logical or analytical thinker) or a right-brainer (more of an expressive or creative thinker), this one is a no-brainer. The time to do this isn't when you're midway through the project, but before you begin. If you want to have a finished manuscript in your hands, *set a deadline*.

HOʻĀʻO: TRY THIS

Decide on a Deadline

Decide on a deadline for a completed first draft (month, day, year):

My deadline for a first draft: _____

HŌʻIKE HOʻOPŌKOLE: CHAPTER SUMMARY

✓ Writing doesn't care if you're dressed in a suit or writing in your pajamas.

✓ Writing is ready when you are, wherever you are.

✓ The key is to start simple.

✓ You're not a writer if you're not writing.

✓ Daily practice can make all the difference in the world.

✓ If you want to write and find that you're having trouble doing so, consider adopting a simple routine that will make writing a regular part of your schedule.

✓ If you want to have a finished manuscript in your hands, set a deadline.

CHAPTER TWO
REMEMBERING

Hoʻomanaʻo

We remember first.

In writing the memoir, our material springs from remembrance. Unlike a biography or autobiography which is based on fact, a memoir is based on memories and moments. It's about an emotional truth, about examining and understanding how something affected us. The value is not in the event itself, but in how it shaped us.

Memoir allows the writer the freedom to choose what to include and what to exclude. It may sound simple, but it's not. Good memoir writing asks that you look at everything that's in front of you, to consider all the relevant material relating to the story you're choosing to tell. That may mean remembering the not-so-good parts about a life, reliving old wounds and hurts, or feeling a twinge of unease when an otherwise cheery memory is interrupted by one that might not be so rosy. Still, all must be considered.

Remember the old song, "Dem Dry Bones?" "Your leg bone's connected to your knee bone / Your knee bone's connected to your thigh bone / Your thigh bone's connected to your hip bone / Your hip bone's connected to your back bone…" and so on. Such it is with memories. Our life is a series of interlinking moments and in isolating a single incident, we can't ignore the other parts still connected to it, even if we want to. They are there, like it or not.

Remembering is an act of courage. It may be heavy or dramatic or emotional at times, but it can also be fun, like digging around for buried treasure. In recalling the first time you sold newspapers to earn money for crack seed to remembering the aunty behind the crack seed counter to the time you saw her in the emergency room where you were both waiting for family members who'd been hurt. It's a thrill to discover long-forgotten memories. You may even be inclined to keep reminiscing and put off the writing (You've been warned!). Here are a few ways to make sure those memories get down on paper.

TOOLS FOR REMEMBERING

Have you ever walked into someone's kitchen and the smell of something simmering on the stove instantly transported you somewhere else? Or maybe you heard a song from many, many years ago and a familiar face or feeling surfaced after years of lying dormant. Such is the power of memory.

Triggers are a fast way to get back into a moment. An old song, a smell, a feeling of déjà vu when you go to a place you've never been to before. These things take us back in time, to a place that no may longer exist except for our memory of it.

There are lots of ways to mine for this gold. Spend an afternoon going through old photos, letters, journals or diary entries. Look at old yearbooks and address books. Rifle through your junk drawer, the boxes stored under the house or in the back of the closet. Poke through your jewelry box. Look through your closet, dump out your purse and wallet, flip through your passport. Scroll through your social media timeline or read old blog posts. Watch old home movies (for those of you with old 8mm projector reels, you may want to get them converted into DVD or digital files). If you find any old family recipes, put on your apron and give one a try.

> *"To recall old memories simply start writing, even if you end up deleting much of it. It's amazing what will come back to you."*
> **PATRICIA JENNINGS**

Ask yourself how you're feeling when you see or experience a trigger. Try to remember what was happening in your life at the time. If it's something you've been holding on to for a while, ask yourself why, and then do it again.

If you're feeling brave and open, call an old friend or relative and ask them about the funniest or saddest memory they have of you, or of your family. Get in touch with an old neighbor—they are less attached to your actions and will have a completely different perspective, most likely one you haven't heard before. Recall a group event (a birthday celebration, a reunion, a retirement party, a baby lūʻau) and contact several people at once, asking them for their most poignant or offbeat memory of that day. Remember, you don't have to use anything anyone gives you. Think of it as a starting off point, a springboard into something else. The story behind the story.

Even if you have an idea about what you want to write, amassing these memories will help uncover more. Your memoir may even take an unexpected turn. You may realize that the story about moving from Osaka to Oʻahu is less about the journey or your new life but what you left behind. A memoir that begins as a love story may really be a story about faith. At this point you'll want to gather all you can so you have plenty of reserves to get you started.

a
b
c
d
e
f
g
h
i
j
k
l
m
n
o
p
q
r
s
t
u
v
w
x
y
z

HOʻĀʻO: TRY THIS

The Alphabet Autobiography

This is a fun and fast way to kick things off. Even if you did this in grade school, chances are things may have changed a bit for you since then. I recommend doing the exercise by hand. Get a sheet of lined paper and write the letters A through Z with one letter per line. Then, beginning with the letter A, describe yourself or a memory that starts with the letter A.

Example: "A is for adamant, because I'm adamant about what I believe in. B is for Betty, my mother-in law, a woman who's a true blessing (Another B!) in my life. C is for careful—I sometimes hold myself back because I'm worried about what other people will think. D is for dancing, something I've never been very good at..." and so on. In writing this example using my own thoughts and memories, I recalled a moment during high school where a girl made fun of the way I danced, imitating me. Alert! Gold ahead! You don't have to get into it now, but you can jot a note and come back to it later. The goal here is to come up with a sentence for each letter of the alphabet, not stopping until you get to Z.

HOʻĀʻO: TRY THIS

"I Remember..."

A first-line prompt that was added to every writer's toolbox by Joe Brainerd, author of *I Remember.* The premise is simple. On a clean sheet of paper, write "I remember" then continue writing whatever comes to mind. The idea is to write without overthinking or analyzing, but to grab the first thought, however random or irrelevant it may seem. When you've gone as far as you can go (sometimes a single sentence, sometimes a whole page), start with another "I remember." I also recommend writing this exercise by hand. It's perfect for people who are having trouble finding time to write. Give yourself five or ten minutes, and go.

HOʻĀʻO: TRY THIS

First Things First
Similar to "I remember," writing about first experiences is an easy
way to go back to the past, fast. Here are a few "firsts" to get you
started—feel free to come up with your own.

Your first car.   The first time you came to Hawaiʻi.

Your first kiss.   The first time you left Hawaiʻi.

Your first boat ride.   The first time someone yelled at you.

Your first airplane ride.   The first time you were scared.

Your first paycheck.   The first time you broke something.

The first time you got into trouble.

HOʻĀʻO: TRY THIS

A Picture is Worth a Thousand Words
Sometimes it helps to "see" what it is you want to write. In addition
to photographs, videos and old documents, try drawing or sketching
your way into your memories.

* Draw the floor plan of a house or apartment you once lived in.

* Draw the floor plan of your office, school, boat, car. Past or present.

* Draw your family tree, going back as far as you can and adding on
  as many branches as possible.

* Draw the island you live on.

* Draw a self-portrait.

HO'Ā'O: TRY THIS

The Bento Box Memoir

Bento boxes are one-person meals divided into a lacquer or plastic box with multiple compartments. Bento boxes have become a bit of an art form lately, neat and tastefully done, sometimes based on a person, place or thing (*oekakiben*). Similar boxed lunches also exist in the Philippines (*baon*), Korea (*dosirak*), Taiwan (*biàndang*) and India (*tiffin*), but in America, it was Hawai'i that made bento boxes the norm.

There are three steps to "assembling" your bento box memoir. First, decide how many compartments (memories). Three is the minimum, six is the maximum. Second, choose a period of time or a theme. A period of time could be a single day (such as a birthday, wedding, first day of school) while a theme focuses on an overall thought, feeling or experience (a list of themes is provided on page 45). Next, dust off your drawing skills by drawing a rectangle or square in the middle of the page. This is your bento box memoir container. Divide your container into the number of compartments you've chosen. Now, fill each compartment with a memory associated with the time or theme you've chosen. Again, you don't want to overthink this. Take the first memory that comes in, even if you're not entirely sure how it's related. Continue until all your compartments are filled.

Example: For my bento box memoir, I am going to have four compartments. I decide on a theme, Arts and Crafts, for no reason other than it stood out on the list and seemed like a fun, no-pressure theme. (Note: Listening to this inner voice will become increasingly more important.)

On a piece of paper, I sketch out a rectangle and four compartments, one big and three small. Then I start thinking. *Arts and crafts, arts and crafts*...I have a dear friend, Mary Spears, who's an artist. I could write about how we met, or how her art makes me feel, the meals she's prepared for me, anything. I start getting distracted but stop myself, and put her name in one box, reassuring myself that I will come back to this later. I start thinking again.

Arts and crafts, arts and crafts...I remember a neighbor on our street when I was seven or eight. She was an elderly woman, single. What was her name? I can't remember. But I would visit and we would make stained-glass ornaments in her oven. I remember dropping in the colored crystals one by one, then waiting excitedly by the oven door for them to melt into smooth glass (which was really plastic). I write that down in another box ("stained glass - neighbor - Houston").

Arts and crafts, arts and crafts...there was a time when we had to draw a self-portrait. As I was drawing it, I thought it was good, but when I looked at my finished picture, I was disappointed. It doesn't feel like there's more there, and I'm not sure that's a good memory. I feel a bit lousy recalling it, actually. *Ding!* It definitely needs to go in. So reluctantly (but trusting the process), I put it in a box, the largest one for some reason ("self portrait - disappointing").

Arts and crafts, arts and crafts...I have an ad hoc "craft room" that is filled with things that once inspired me but now I feel overwhelmed by it. Yet I can't throw any of it away. Wait, what kind of memory is that? That's not a memory. It's a random feeling, and not a great one at that. I don't get how it's related at all. And yet I feel it lingering as I try to think of something else. Okay, fine. I'll include it. There's a flash and I remember the hope and excitement I felt when I was first accumulating the buttons and ink pads and beads. I write "current craft room - stuff - overwhelmed - buttons - ink pads - eBay - beads - hope" and realize I'd thrown in eBay. That's right, I'd bought a lot of stuff at auction, including some batches of supplies that held surprises when I received them.

Now that each of my compartments is filled, I go back and start jotting more notes and memories associated with each compartment. Usually three to five bullet points per compartment is enough. So when I go to the compartment with Mary, I add "birds of paradise - Hawaiian Sun - slippahs - hospital." That's what comes; I still don't have to figure it all out just yet. For the stained glass memory, I add "Girl Scout cookies - happy - Shari." For self-portrait I add "horses - hair - Chinese association newsletter - grocery store - Dad." (I just got a big *ding* with that one. But moving on...) Finally, for craft room, I write "paper - color - possibilities - expertise - Upcountry Studio." Keep going through each compartment until you feel like you've shook it all out.

When you're done, look at all of it. Stick it up on your wall, let it sit overnight. When you're ready, look at your bento box and circle a key word or phrase from each compartment. For me, that's *birds of paradise, stained glass, hope,* and *Dad.* Already a memory surfaces of a time my father took a class and made a stained-glass panel of ducks and pussywillows and long blades of grass. I start writing. I remember seeing it for the first time on the kitchen table in our house in Houston, remember how the cool Mexican tile felt below my feet on an otherwise sweltering day. I know (from having gone back to this period of time before) that our days in Houston were formative for me, so I know these bits and pieces are important even if I don't understand (yet) how it all connects.

If I really want to go deep with this, I can ask my father about it. It's not about telling his story, but clarifying my own understanding of why this memory still lurks. (My own take: It was one of the first times I recall my father engaged in making something.)

The best thing about the bento box memoir is that you can go back to the same box and find another memory by circling new words that catch your attention. Again, this exercise is about triggers, not precision or adhering to any original idea or thought. Come up with as many bento boxes as you can (more ambitious writers can start at the top of the list of themes and make a bento box for each one).

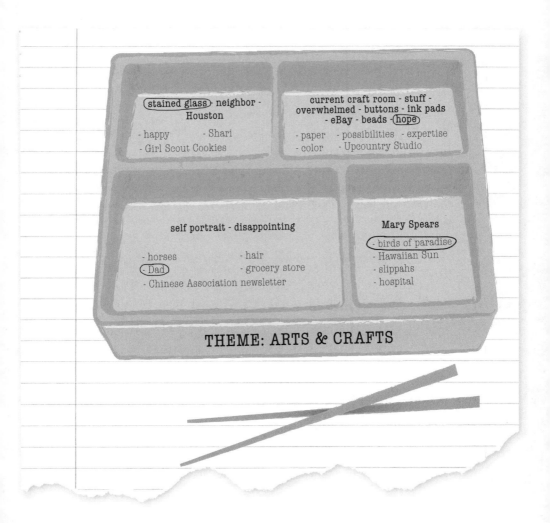

(stained glass) - neighbor -
Houston

- happy   - Shari
- Girl Scout Cookies

current craft room - stuff -
overwhelmed - buttons - ink pads
- eBay - beads - (hope)

- paper   - possibilities - expertise
- color   - Upcountry Studio

self portrait - disappointing

- horses   - hair
- (Dad)   - grocery store
- Chinese Association newsletter

Mary Spears

- birds of paradise
- Hawaiian Sun
- slippahs
- hospital

THEME: ARTS & CRAFTS

HO'Ā'O: TRY THIS

The Six-Word Memoir
The Six-Word Memoir® is the brainchild of SMITH *Magazine* (sixwordmemoirs.com). The goal is simple: Write your memoir in exactly six words, no more, no less. You can't break up compound words but you can play with contractions ("do not" = two words, "don't" = one word). Their tagline sums it up: *One life. Six words. What's yours?*™

Here are some six-word memoirs from some of my students:

"Born on O'ahu, raised on Hawai'i." (Kai Ibana)

"Got hit, life bit, rage quit." (Taran Takahashi)

"I live clean and surf mean." (Kamuela Spencer-Herring)

"All my scars are my stories." (Ryan Hooley)

"Roping wild cattle is a battle." (Levi Higa)

"Determination is fuel for a journey." (Christian Gomez)

"Perfect timing. I should have known." (Arielle Faith Michael)

"Polynesian, Oriental, European, all in one." (George Manu)

"He loved me but left anyway." (Elsbeth McKeen)

Take a 3"x5" index card and on the lined side, see how many six-word memoirs you can come up with in five minutes. Then choose the best one and write it on the blank side of the card. Tape it somewhere nearby to keep you inspired.

SIFTING

If you get good at remembering, chances are you'll end up with more than you need. Information may start coming in from all directions, some of it junk, some of it not. It may start to overwhelm you, or maybe even feel impossible. What are you supposed to do with all these details that don't seem to go anywhere or do anything?

A couple of years ago my husband and I cleaned out his parents' garage so it would be safer and easier for them to find things. We had a finite amount of time, plus the large thirty-foot dumpster sitting on the driveway was an eyesore. We had to figure out what to keep, what to give away, what to discard.

Over fifty years of married life were crammed (very efficiently) into that two-car garage. My husband and I thought we could go in with an objective eye and get through everything quickly, but that was of course impossible. He found a monogrammed towel that belonged to the grandfather he never met. My father-in-law's army fatigues still hung in a makeshift closet. Buckets of old golf balls bore the names of golf courses they had played. Boxes of Christmas decorations harkened back to my husband's childhood. An

> *"Sifting informs the writer. That is its purpose."*
> **CHRIS VANDERCOOK**

old transistor radio sat dusty in the corner of a work bench (the garage was my father-in-law's escape whenever he wanted a little peace and quiet). A former professor, my father-in-law had boxes of notes and exams from when he used to teach in New York and later California. We even found a car bumper from my brother-in-law's Volkswagen Golf GTI. It had been lost among the eaves of the garage, obscured by cardboard and planks of wood and a couple of old bean bags. It had been there for almost thirty years, unbeknownst to all of us.

The bottom line was this: Almost every item in that garage had a story, down to the last nail.

What we thought would take three days took five. Many of the things we found my in-laws had forgotten about, but once they saw them, they couldn't let them go. One of my most vivid memories (and one we joke about now) is of my mother-in-law clutching three silverplate ice buckets that she insisted she still needed even though she had forgotten she ever owned them. She literally body blocked me (still holding those ice buckets) when I uncovered two full tea service sets that she hadn't seen in decades. That garage was full of triggers to their past and, by extension, the past of my husband and children. How could we just throw it all away?

We sifted through every item. We filled that dumpster to overflowing and still had a garage full of things. But what we chose to keep—and what my in-laws agreed to let go of—took on new meaning. Old stories and memories were resurrected. Sifting through everything was an arduous process, but it was also how we came to remember the past. We discovered that once the stories were told, my in-laws were ready to release many of the things because we took the time to talk about them, to listen.

Every memory is an opportunity for more. *This is a good thing.* Don't stop because it feels like too much. If it feels overwhelming, use the tools in the Getting Started section to schedule the time you put aside for working on your memoir and stick to it. When time is up, let your attention return to the demands of your daily life. Being able to shift in and out of working on your memoir will make the process more enjoyable.

Remember that the act of sifting through old memories and moments isn't just about organizing your thoughts or choosing the right stories for your memoir. It's about putting yourself in a place where you are receptive to more. It's about developing a sharper sense for what really mattered in a particular moment. Your polished memoir will reflect this focus and hard work.

Be willing to go there, to push through feelings of unease or discomfort to get to the heart of a memory. You're peeling the onion, layer by layer. Don't be surprised if there are a few tears.

When you've finished sifting, you should have a strong idea of what the story or stories are that you want to tell. The theme of your memoir should be evident. You might even know the order in which events will be presented (remember, it doesn't have to be chronological). You may feel like you have too much or not enough. Keep sifting. Keep sifting until you feel like it's time to write.

WHEN MEMORY DIFFERS FROM THE FACTS

Maybe that important day you want to write about is fuzzy around the edges. Maybe you thought it was summertime, but it might have been spring or fall. Maybe a story you've told for years gets corrected at a family reunion—no, Uncle Pinky didn't tell that joke, Cousin Noa did. What do you do now?

If you're writing a memoir, you have an obligation to the reader to be as accurate as possible. Don't guess, don't embellish. We are trusting you to share your truth as closely and authentically as possible. If you're writing a biography, you have a duty to fact check your information. If you're interviewing someone and their recollection differs from the facts (dates or places, or example), sometimes the simplest thing to do is to disclose the discrepancy.

> *"First of all, what is fact? To what extent is everything we know about history truly factual? History is as much about perspective and perception as it is about fact and truth."*
> **WARREN NISHIMOTO**

Memories are sometimes layers or even collages of different events or people, meshed into one—memories don't always abide by the rules. Your job as the writer is to gently untangle what's tangled and see what you've got.

Cross-reference your memories with your calendar, check with others who may have been there, too. It's not about gathering their memories, but double-checking the small details that are important to your story, in the very least for scene, setting and timing. After all, you want to make sure the place the six green sea turtles that swam up alongside you was Kiholo Bay and not Kiʻilae Bay. If the location is not important or you can't confirm, you always have the option of keeping it generic ("At a beach on the island of Hawaiʻi in 2002, I was free diving when six green sea turtles swam up beside me."). It's important not to mislead and just as important not to be too lazy. Good writing, be it fiction or nonfiction, requires your best efforts, your every attention.

Tell the stories of your life as you remember it, but corroborate what you can. If you find a discrepancy, Leslie Lang suggests referring to the difference right in the text: "I remember it being red, and am surprised when I look at pictures now and see that it was yellow." Billy Bergin, who writes biographies, does the same. "When memory conflicts with facts, I report both."

A good rule of thumb is that if someone else, given a little time and energy, can uncover the truth (or untruth) of what you wrote, so can you. Gail Miyasaki warns that subjects, including ourselves, may edit parts of our lives that may be unflattering or embarrassing. Be careful. There are plenty of writers who've been called on the liberties they've taken in their memoirs. Do your best not to be one of them, if not for the simple reason that you don't want what's good and important in your work to be colored by a few loose details you didn't bother to clean up.

FINDING YOUR STORY

So now that you've looked at what you have to work with (and know that more will continue to come), how do you find your story?

Some of you may already know what you want to write about. You may have been thinking about it for years, or people have been telling you that you should write down the story of your life. Maybe your memoir will be about one special summer or maybe it spans several decades of your life. It could be about a single event, such as swimming the Moloka'i channel, or

> *"A memoir or biography is still storytelling, so it needs to be a really good story."*
> **STUART HOLMES COLEMAN**

the search for your birth parents. It could even be a collection of funny family anecdotes or a time when you ate your way through Honolulu. With memoir, the possibilities are endless.

If you aren't sure exactly what you want to write about, that's sometimes the best place to start. It means you're open to seeing where the story leads you, to writing about what wants to be noticed or acknowledged. What starts out as a story about childhood trauma may end up about how hula saved you. What might seem like a small thing—a visit to the observatories at the top of Mauna Kea—may lead you to the story of how you reconciled with your estranged brother. Look through your writing, your diaries, your photos, your social media posts, your most prized possessions. The idea is to follow the thread that calls to you, to choose the one that seems to have the most energy, the most juice, the most fun or intrigue. It could also be the memory you want desperately to avoid, the one that makes you cringe when you think of it, the one you don't want to remember but still can't forget.

There are no lives too boring or too "normal." Even if you don't feel like you've had a life-changing experience or lived off the land or survived a tsunami (or two), start writing from wherever you are and see what comes to the surface. You may be surprised at how powerful the memories and moments of your life actually are.

The power of memoir is in the truth of a story. Readers will resonate with this truth and some may even be affected or changed by it. Writing your story (or stories) is not only fun and rewarding, but in some cases can free you. We are called to live authentically and express our true selves through our action and our words. Sharing your story, be it with a friend or through publication, invites others to look at your life through their own lens and find their own connection. This is how we grow, by interacting and learning from one another. In no place is this more evident than in memoir.

HŌʻIKE HOʻOPŌKOLE: CHAPTER SUMMARY

✓ Memoir allows the writer the freedom to choose what to include and what to exclude.

✓ Our life is a series of interlinking moments.

✓ Triggers are a fast way to get back into a moment.

✓ Every memory is an opportunity for more.

✓ If it feels overwhelming, use the tools in the Getting Started section to schedule the time you put aside for working on your memoir and stick to it.

✓ You have an obligation to the reader to be as accurate as possible.

✓ Tell the stories of your life as you remember it, but corroborate what you can.

✓ The power of memoir is in the truth of a story.

CHAPTER THREE
WRITING

- - - - - - - - - - - - - - -

Kākau

N ow that you know what you're writing about, it's time to put pen to paper or fingers to the keyboard. It's easier said than done, I know. It's one thing to say you want to write a memoir, and another thing to actually have to do it.

Have faith. You didn't get this far without having an inkling of where you want to go. You know the story that will emerge, so now we just need to figure out how. The craft of memoir writing is more than a jumble of words on a page, especially if you hope to share or publish your work. There are plenty of great books that teach the elements of writing, and a few of my favorites are listed in the back of this book. Whether a new or seasoned author, you will always be asked to sharpen your skills. Any job requires a certain degree of continuing education, and it's no different here.

You can always just start writing, but I'd like to help save you some time down the road by asking you to consider a few key elements first. A memoir is not an extended journal entry. It is not a collection of random writing exercises. A well-written memoir is the result of a set of deliberate choices (made by you) about what to share and how to share it. Pacing and momentum are critical to ensure that the reader stays engaged. There are details that may be interesting and wonderful but irrelevant to the core story and you may have to make the difficult decision of leaving them out. Knowing what to keep and what to keep out can make all the difference.

Memoirs are often referred to as creative nonfiction, which means that while it's based on a true story, it's presented as a story in the same way fiction is. Therefore the basic elements of fiction—characters, plot and story arc, details, language—apply to the memoir as well. Most nonfiction books are notorious for delivering information in a dry, almost report-like manner, but memoirs are meant to lift readers from their lives and have them follow you on your journey. It is a form of entertainment and escape as much as it is information.

There are no hard and fast rules about what a memoir should look like or how it needs to be structured. Memoirists push these limits every day. There is room to be creative and explore how your story will look on a page. But as with all things, it helps to know how some of these pieces tend to fit together best, to look at other successful memoirs and see how they were written. When I say "successful," I am talking about a memoir that a reader picks up and is unable to put down. They read it all the way through to the end, not because they are your friend or related to you, but because the writing is good and you've engaged them and connected with them. You've made them want to read more. Then, when they get to the end, they close the book and take a deep breath and think (or say), "That was a good story." That, in my opinion, is a successful memoir.

THE CHARACTERS IN THE STORY OF YOUR LIFE

Our experiences are affected by the people who are a part of our lives—including those who have been absent—and the choices we make in response to these people. When writing your memoir, you'll need to know who these key people are and, more importantly, who the main character is.

In literature, the main character is known as the protagonist. If you're writing a memoir, the protagonist is you. You are, for obvious reasons, the most important character in your story. It goes without saying that readers will fall in love with you, right?

Maybe. Maybe not.

How a character is portrayed and introduced to a reader is paramount, especially if that character is you. Readers tend to identify closely with the protagonist—they become emotionally invested, they want to know what will happen. Readers will attach to your stories and your journey, especially because these stories are true. What keeps them turning the page is the desire to find out what hap-

> *"But exactly who tells the tale, recounts the memory, invents that life?"*
> **BOB BUSS**

pened to you and whether or not you turned out okay in the end—physically, emotionally, spiritually. Have you ever read a book or saw a movie where you knew that everything would work out in the end, and yet you still wanted to read or watch, just to make sure?

Readers relate to the main character in one of two ways: empathy or sympathy. With empathy, readers feel what the main character feels; they know what it's like or have gone through something similar. With sympathy, readers are looking in from the outside, witnessing events and connecting with the humanity of the situation, but not necessarily able to put themselves in the main character's shoes.

Since the reader doesn't know you (yet), you need to make sure you introduce yourself to them. Some details you'll want to offer right away are:

* Physical description
* What motivates you, or what's important to you, or why you're telling this story
* How things may change for you during the course of your memoir

Since you will be narrating your own story, there's a tendency to assume that how you feel about something or a choice you would make is obvious to the reader. It's not. We don't know enough about you to know who you are or what you will do, but we also don't want to read through pages of backstory to figure it out. Instead, drop us right into a situation so we can see you in action. Show us what's going on around you and what you are doing in response, how you're feeling. Are you angry, did you throw a book out the window? Did you stare at your shoes and count to ten? Did you go home and make a vow never to let anyone get the better of you again? Did your face get hot, did people laugh, did you want to disappear?

We can get a physical description of you, too, through the voice of other people. "My mother always said my hair was too black," or "The kids in school used to laugh that I was left-handed." Saying that you were Miss Kona Coffee says more than "Some people think I'm pretty." As superficial as some of these descriptions may be, if they are true and add another dimension to your character, consider including them. Let other people in your story do the work for you, though we do want to know how you see yourself, too.

Another important thing to remember is that we are trusting you. We are trusting you to be honest in your portrayal of yourself and others. Readers can tell if you're embellishing or hiding something or skimming the surface. The temptation to paint ourselves in a favorable light is only human—in fact, we're asked to do this very thing whenever we apply for schools or jobs, whenever we interview or meet new people. But no one is perfect and I personally have little interest in reading stories about someone who is. We want the whole picture of the person we're dealing with, warts and all. You have to be willing to reveal things that might be embarrassing or even painful if the story calls for it.

We want to see (and understand) your bad choices just as much as your good ones. Don't feel like you have to clean it up and make it pretty, no matter how tempting. We all know how messy real life can be, and life stories are a way of sharing with others how you made it through (so they can, too). When you let yourself and your characters be real on the page, you enhance, not diminish, what you went through.

"One of your missions," Mark Panek tells us, "is to create empathetic characters that your readers will root for." Who else is in your story? We need to get to know them, too. Share a moment with us that reveals who they are by something they do or say. If your older brother Keoki was the equivalent of the town drunk, show us a scene or two where we can see Keoki drunk through your eyes, making one bad choice after another. Let us form our opinions alongside you and then let us be there on the day when everything changed. Show us what he did the day the tsunami hit—how he was the first one evacuating neighbors, carrying children on his back and rescuing people from cars. When you tell us later that he quit drinking, finished his GED and then applied for the police academy, we'll know how significant and monumental the moment is when he received his badge at the age of forty.

And maybe the story isn't really about Keoki. Maybe it's about you, but it's easier to write about him, because he was (and is) so heroic. You're just plain old boring you who panicked at the last minute and tried to save your photo albums even as people were screaming for help. Some writers may find it difficult to write about themselves and some might even feel that they are insignificant compared to an event or life-changing situation they were in. But remember that people read memoirs not so much to know about how destructive tsunamis can be, but the havoc the tsunami may have wrecked on your life. How did it affect you, both in the moment and after? How did it change you?

No one has lived your life. Let us in so we can see what it was like.

HO‘Ā‘O: TRY THIS

The Author Bio
This is a fun exercise to do at the beginning of the writing process and warms you up to the idea of writing about yourself. In seventy-five words or less, write the author biography that you would like to see on your memoir's book jacket or in the back of the book. Remember to write it in the third person. You'll find that most author bios are filled with accolades and credentials, but even if you've never been published before I bet you can find something worth sharing. Check out the author bios in the About the Experts section in the back of this book for ideas.

HOʻĀʻO: TRY THIS

The Author Profile Page
Have you ever seen celebrity or reader profiles in your favorite magazine? This exercise involves a little creativity. Place your favorite picture of yourself in the middle of the page, and then write one to two sentences highlighting your favorite things (favorite book, movie, food, quote, vacation spot, item of clothing, room in the house, etc.). Other fun things include a secret talent, morning routine, why you love your job, what inspires you, the best piece of advice you ever received. Make sure your profile page is representative of you, so that anyone who knew you well would nod their head and agree. "Yep, that's you all right!" Throw a curve ball or two, something that only you know but feel ready to share. Keep this exercise fun and light, focusing on what you love and want to celebrate.

HOʻĀʻO: TRY THIS

Three Words
Talk about revealing! In this exercise, what three words would you use to describe yourself to:

* A potential employer
* A landlord
* A blind date or future lover
* A classroom full of children
* Your grandchildren
* The president of the United States

More often than not, you'll find yourself using different words to describe yourself to different people. Which words appear to be consistent?

HO'Ā'O: TRY THIS

The Pua Petal Character Technique

This is a great way to quickly establish the key influencers in your life. Take a piece of paper and draw a circle in the middle. Put your name inside (if you're married, you can put either your maiden name or your married name—each may yield different responses). You can also put a photograph of you from any time of your life in the center. Then, draw eight large petals around the circle (sometimes it helps to draw a petal at 12:00, 3:00, 6:00 and 9:00, and then fill in the rest).

When you think about the people in your life, or those who've influenced you in any way, who comes to mind? They can be family, friends, enemies, co-workers or neighbors, it doesn't matter. If you're feeling stuck, stare at your own name or photograph, then write the first name that comes to mind regardless of how odd or unrelated they may seem. Add one detail about them. Write until all eight petals are full. If you fill all eight petals and want to replace someone, cross their name out with one line (don't erase) and write in the new name. The reason for this is that you may want to come back to that initial person later.

Now choose a petal and write about that person for ten minutes. It can about your relationship, something that happened, a description of that person or how you came to know them. For ten minutes, write as much as you can. Do this for each petal around the flower (you can also break this up and write one petal a day). After you've done all eight petals, write for ten minutes about the person (you) in the center. It doesn't matter what you write—we're just warming up our writing muscles and seeing what's out there.

Your flower may look something like this. →

PLOT

Don't let the word "plot" throw you off—our everyday lives exist on plots. Plots are the story behind the story and your memoir needs one.

When writers talk about plot, they're usually talking about a sequence of events that build to a climax and then get resolved. Also included are antagonists—the people or things that oppose you and cause conflict. Antagonists are often interpersonal and may be family or people close to you (though not necessarily). The old adage that the people who know you best are often the ones that can inflict the most damage is certainly the case with most antagonists, but it can also be anyone who threatens to stand in the way of you getting what you want or need.

A plot is not just a device used to engage a reader. Plot is about the journey, both external (you really wanted to be accepted into that Japanese exchange program in Tokyo but competition was fierce) and internal (you wanted it because you thought it would help gain approval from your Japanese father who abandoned you at birth). You may think that you're writing about moving to Maui and living off the grid, but maybe the real story is about what

> *"It's not about me; it's about what I have discovered and learned and gained understanding of."*
> **DAVID ULRICH**

you left behind, maybe even who you left behind, and why. It may turn out that what you were moving to was really more about what you were moving from. As the writer, you need to figure out what your story is really about. Once you have that figured out, you continue to build on your memoir by identifying the causality of each event.

The definition of causality is the relationship between an event (the cause) and a second event (the effect), in which the second event occurred as a consequence of the first. In other words, something caused something else to happen. A trip to the bank holds little interest to a reader. A trip to the bank and being caught in the middle of a holdup is interesting, but it's not enough—we want more. A trip to the bank and being caught in the middle of a holdup and deciding to overpower the perpetrators, hide or run away (and then what happens as a result of that decision) is a memoir.

Another example: You go to the store to buy a loaf of bread. Who cares, right? But if you went to the store to buy a loaf of bread and came back with a three-tiered wedding cake instead, you'd have our attention. If we then found out the cake cost $250, we'd be asking if you were *lōlō* but still, then, we'd want to know more. When you tell us that today would have been your twenty-fifth wedding anniversary if you had married the man you loved but your parents made you cancel the wedding on the day of, we are now officially hooked.

To recap, plot is the who, what, how and why of life. Plot is about the hard decisions we make and the reasons behind them. Plot is about happiness, power, revenge or success and what we're willing to do to get it. Plot is the blueprint of any life story, however short or long. Know your plot, and we're putty in your hands.

Remember that an event itself, however momentous, is not what makes the memoir. We did not pick up your book to read about the event but what you did in response to that event, how it changed you or didn't. There are no easy answers out there. Our choices, our awareness, our regrets, our joys, our understanding of what we would do differently or wish we had a chance to do again...*that's* what makes a memoir.

HOʻĀʻO: TRY THIS

Playing with Plots
Even though plot is a part of our everyday life, it's a boring mechanical term that throws people off. These exercises will help you practice writing and recognizing plot lines so you can better see them in your own life:

✳ Outline a story between a husband and wife whose marriage is on the rocks. The husband has cancer but is refusing treatment; the wife is distraught. Describe them in detail. Write down three possible outcomes.

✳ A young woman moves in next door with only one suitcase and five boxes. She begins looking for a job the next day. Describe her in detail. Fast forward three months and write down three possible outcomes.

✳ Two men are sitting next to each other at a bar when they notice they both have the same tattoo on their inside left wrist. They begin talking and discover that they have the same basic body type, hair color, nose. They are two years apart in age, both only children to adoptive parents. Write down three possible outcomes.

✳ Think of a novel you recently read or a movie you recently saw. Who were the main characters, what key events occurred, what challenges or mishaps happened and how was it resolved? How did the characters change (or not)? Did anything happen that was unexpected or surprising? Was there any foreshadowing?

THE STORY ARC

If plot is about causality and *why*, then story arc is the map that leads the way. It's about *how* the reader experiences what you write about. Story arcs are like signs along the road, pointing the reader in the right direction. There are lots of ways to do this, and the simplest way is the three-act structure.

Act One is the beginning, the basic setup where we meet you and get a sense for what your life was like before the event or series of events that occur. It's an introduction, but it's also where we meet the other people in your story and learn about your values. Act One usually ends with the event that changes everything or sets the memoir in action. At this point the reader should be fully drawn into your story and wanting to know more.

Act Two is the middle which usually comprises the bulk of your memoir. It's when we see how you navigate the stormy waters. These challenges do not have easy answers and oftentimes one problem is resolved only to have another appear. There's a sense of tension. Something is at stake. The story is building to an outcome that we might be anxious about but can't look away just the same. We have no choice but to read on because while we can feel everything pointing to a resolution, we're not sure what it is and we are desperate to find out.

> *"Lives don't always follow an ideal dramatic arc. Few have a Hollywood ending, and too many end in a slow decline."*
> **CHRIS VANDERCOOK**

Act Three is the end, the peak of the crisis (also known as the climax) where you face the real and final lesson. As things taper off, there's usually an aha moment, an acceptance or realization of how things now are. In a way you've come full circle. You are different than when your story began, and you have the memoirist's ability to reflect on what it all means. As a reader, we reach the same conclusion you do by virtue of the fact that we've been paying attention and following along. Your triumph (or new awareness) is ours, too.

Life, however, is rarely this neat. Applying the three-act structure (or eight-point arc, another popular structure) to a real-life event doesn't always work. At this point you'll need to ask yourself if the problem is with the structure or your story? It may take some work to write your story into a three-act structure, such as excluding a fun detail or anecdote that may sidetrack the story or including a betrayal you'd hope to gloss over or avoid altogether. This is the challenge every memoirist faces, to get to the heart of what's really going on.

But what if you genuinely can't get it to work? What if there is no Act Three, no climax, no aha moment? Maybe it was just a snapshot of a time in your life or you just want to get the details of your life down on paper. If that's what it is, then what? Is all this structure stuff really necessary?

If you are writing your memoir to share or to publish, structure is important. Readers are looking for a rhythm in your work. They want to be carried away and changed. If you don't change in your story, neither will they. Most events of consequence naturally follow a three-act structure. It's up to you to determine what those events are. As Lee Cataluna says, "The structure should grow from the story itself."

So draw the reader in, keep the reader engaged and leave them with a sense of completion or satisfaction at the end. Structure helps you keep your focus and know what to include/exclude, but if you are able to forgo it and can still bring a reader to the end of your story with a smile on their face or a satisfied sigh, you've done your job.

THEMES

Themes inform the reader what your memoir is about so they know what to expect. When readers peruse the shelves, they tend to be looking for a certain kind of story. You don't want somebody to be unhappy with what they read not because the story or writing wasn't good, but because it wasn't what they expected. Someone looking for a coming-of-age memoir involving bulimia is going to be disappointed if it turns out to be about the old war days or the time you

> *"The human element is the thread that runs through successful memoirs. It's this human aspect that draws readers to memoirs."*
> **FRANCES KAKUGAWA**

won a surfing competition at the age of forty. It's not that your story isn't riveting—it's just not what they were looking for.

It's also helpful for you to know the theme of your memoir. In many cases multiple themes may exist but it's important to narrow the focus to one or two—you'll need to resist the impulse to include everything but the kitchen sink. Remember: You can write many different memoirs about your life, but you want each one to have a clear theme, the one that's at the heart of your memoir.

HERE ARE A FEW THEMES TO CONSIDER:

Abandonment

Abuse

Accepting Change

Accidents

Activism

Addiction

Adoption

Anger

Appearances

Arts and Crafts

Being Gifted

Belonging

Betrayal

Bravery

Bullies

Call to Hawaiʻi

Censorship

Challenges

Change

Childhood

Coming of Age

Commitment

Communication

Community

Cooperation

Coping with Loss

Courage and Honor

Cultural Diversity

Customs and Traditions

Dance

Death and Dying

Dementia

Discrimination

Diversity

Divorce

Dreams

Environment

Ethical Dilemmas

Euthanasia

Faith

Family

Fear

Forgiveness

Freedom

Friendship

Gender Issues

Good vs. Evil

Gratitude

Grief

Growing Up

Guilt

Handicaps

Hawaiian Heritage

Heroism

History

Honesty

Hope

Humor

Identity

Immigration

Initiation

Innocence

Intergenerational Relationships

Invincibility

Jealousy

Jobs

Leadership

Lifestyle Change

Living Abroad

Loneliness

Loss

Love

Loyalty

Making Choices

Marriage

Media

Moving

Nature

Nostalgia

Patriotism

Peace

Peer Pressure

Political Issues

Poverty

Preservation

Rebirth

Relationships

Religion

Science

Self-Esteem

Sense of Self

Separation

Social Change

Spirituality

Survival

Taking a Stand

Teamwork

Travel

Trust

War

DETAILS, DETAILS, DETAILS

Details provide proof. They provide a level of description that shows the reader that this person or place is real. Details add life to a story and help create a mental picture in the minds of readers. Have you ever heard someone talk enthusiastically about a place and feel like you were there? You could almost see it, smell it, touch it, taste it. Good writing takes the reader there so they are able to participate in the moment.

"Include details, and go deeper. How did the thing you're remembering look, feel, sound, smell or taste? What did it always remind you of? How did your great-aunt always describe it? Looking back, did it fall into some sort of pattern or theme of your life? What is important about it?"
LESLIE LANG

"Let the story tell the story," Frances Kakugawa tells us. "Not the writer." In other words, show, don't tell. Let the reader experience the story so they become a part of the story.

You can tell us your grandfather had bad teeth, or you can show us your grandfather had bad teeth by describing the way strangers would cringe when he opened his mouth, the dentist shaking his head, the expression on your grandfather's face when he bit into an apple and it hurt. When you paint a picture with good details, we not only see it, we can feel what's happening as a result. Revulsion. Embarrassment. Discomfort. Hopelessness.

You can tell us how excited the kids were when the ice cream truck turned down your street, or you can describe how front doors would fly open and children would stream out, nickels and quarters and dollars in hand, some zipping their pants as if they'd been going to the bathroom when they heard the familiar cheery tune of the ice cream truck.

Details are the cream of a story—they enrich your memoir. You can have two people writing about the same event, even experiencing a similar range of emotions, but it will be the details that help one story stand out from another.

HOʻĀʻO: TRY THIS

Show and Tell
Take these "tell" statements and "show" us instead:

* Aunty was crying.
* Kui was angry.
* Lani had long hair.
* The neighbor's dog was annoying.
* Tūtū was jealous.
* My teacher was too tall.
* The building was run down.

HOʻĀʻO: TRY THIS

Use Your Senses
For ten minutes, describe any of the following using each of your five senses (taste, touch, smell, sight, sound):

* Your bank
* The smells coming from your kitchen
* Eating saimin
* The line in the grocery story
* A pet or animal in or around your home

PLACE

Where does your story take place? Is the place even important?

You may not think so, especially if your story jumps around or focuses on a pivotal relationship or event, but the place (or setting) tells us more than you realize. It sets the stage and informs the reader about how things looked and felt through your eyes. In some cases, it gives us a sense of foreshadowing; in other cases, additional information. Were you at home or at the beach when your spouse called off the marriage? Were you at a lū'au, surrounded by people? Or sitting at the airport in those hard plastic chairs when the text arrived over your phone, announcing the break up? Memoirists can draw parallels between the place they're in and what's happening to them—the cold, impersonal feel of a hospital may compound their loneliness, the sterility of their situation. As a writer you don't need to reach too far to draw these conclusions—they're often there, whether we realize it or not.

> *"Give a clear picture of where it takes place."*
> **PATRICIA JENNINGS**

Details are important when it comes to describing a place. If your family went on a summer vacation and ended up staying in a hotel, describe the hotel. After all, not all hotels are created equal. One with rusty locks on the door and bars on the windows, screaming neighbors and a broken TV is quite different from one with a well-stocked mini bar, an ocean view and room service. Describe the hotel you were in so we know what it was like. If the carpet felt spongy under your feet or you had to share three threadbare towels with your parents and siblings, we get an idea of how you might be feeling or how the vacation was shaping up. Set the stage so we are standing right next to you as you tell your story.

HOʻĀʻO: TRY THIS

Where Are You?
For fifteen minutes, write about one of the following. If it's a place you have access to, go and sit in the space and write. Otherwise work from memory.

* Describe your bedroom

* Describe the last restaurant you had breakfast, lunch or dinner in

* Describe the inside of your car

* Describe a locker room

* Describe the last airplane you were on

* Describe your favorite place to swim

HOʻĀʻO: TRY THIS

List It
Lists are a great way to get the details down quickly. Don't worry if you're getting it right or wrong, don't worry if you're forgetting something important. Write a one-page list of:

* Places you've eaten in the past year. This can be restaurants, cafés, friends' houses, church potlucks, the beach, etc.

* Places you've gone on vacation

* Places you've lived

* Places that remind you of an ex

* Places you dislike

* The furniture, fixtures and items in your living room

* The furniture, fixtures and items in your kitchen

* The furniture, fixtures and items in your primary bathroom

* Places you love in the town or city you live. This can be stores, the park, the school, the post office, the old movie theatre, etc.

DIALOGUE AND LANGUAGE

Since memoir is often written in a narrative form similar to a novel, dialogue plays an important role. Dialogue is another tool in your toolbox that helps move the story forward and imparts additional information to the reader. It breaks up long stretches of backstory and exposition. Sometimes a single exchange of dialogue can do more than an entire paragraph of lengthy explanation.

Dialogue is also important because it gives the reader a chance to hear voices other than your own. We are able to visualize someone faster if we can "hear" how they talk. The key to good dialogue is reading it aloud. Good dialogue shouldn't sound stilted or unnatural. Dialogue works well with physical mannerisms as well. When we can see what someone says and how their body reacted, we have more information about that person.

> *"Stay authentic, but accessible with language."*
> **GAIL MIYASAKI**

You can write:
She said it smelled funny.

Or put it in dialogue:
"That smells funny," she said.

With dialogue, you can throw in other details as well:
"That smells funny," she said, wrinkling her nose.
"That smells funny," she said, pinching her nose with two fingers.
"That smells funny," she said, backing away.

When using quotation marks, any punctuation goes inside the closing quotation mark, and the pronoun is always lower case (unless it's "I" or a proper noun, like Frank or Sue).

NO: "I'll have a loco moco and decaf", she said.
NO: "I'll have a loco moco and decaf." She said.
YES: "I'll have a loco moco and decaf," she said.

When writing the memoir, writing dialogue is tricky in that nobody carried around a tape recorder to capture exactly what was said, word for word. You remember Uncle saying that, but did he say it in that way? Who can remember a conversation from twenty, thirty or fifty years ago (much less last week)? What obligation do we have in ensuring that what was said *was* actually said?

Fortunately, this otherwise grey area follows some basic guidelines. Because all memoirists face this dilemma, it's generally accepted that dialogue is representative and not a verbatim account. If the essence of what is said is accurately represented, that is what matters. In writing the memoir, you are writing the truth as closely as you can get to it, and that includes in dialogue as well. If you'd rather not risk anyone accusing you of misrepresenting their words, you can consider excluding dialogue from your memoir but be aware that (1) these same people may accuse you of misrepresenting their words whether or not it's in dialogue or written into the narrative and (2) it's difficult to honestly write a memoir if you are worried about what others will think. If your memoir contains information that could be construed as libel or false information, then consult with a lawyer or find another way to share the information. The point here is not to get paranoid (though plenty of people do, usually to their own detriment). Remember that your memoir has a larger theme, a larger intention and purpose. There are many ways to tell your story, and how you use dialogue (or choose not to) is up to you.

Learning to write dialogue takes some getting used to, but once you get started, chances are you'll love it. It's fun, and you can see how the story suddenly feels alive. Study up on different speech verbs (said, choked, smiled, laughed, joked). More importantly, read both novels and memoirs so you can see how dialogue works in different ways.

HOʻAʻO: TRY THIS

What Did They Say?

Warm up your dialogue muscles by trying any of these exercises:

* Write, in dialogue, a discussion you had this morning between yourself and another person. When you're finished, be sure to read it aloud to hear how it sounds. You'll be surprised at the errors you'll catch!

* Eavesdrop the next time you're at the store. When you get home, write down the conversation in dialogue.

* Remember a recent argument you had with someone. Write down the argument in dialogue.

* Make up a dialogue between two women exercising at the gym.

* Make up a dialogue between two men fishing off the rocks.

* Make up a dialogue between a mother and a daughter arguing about the daughter's boyfriend.

What if you or the people in your memoir speak pidgin? In Hawaiian, pidgin is a form of communication that literally means hard-taro or pounding taro speech (*ʻolelo paʻi ʻai*). It's simple, raw and undiluted, often having adapted words from other languages such as Chinese, Japanese, Tagalog or Portuguese. It was a way for people from different languages to speak together. It's phonetically-based, which means that it's spelled like it sounds.

Writing pidgin in dialogue can be powerful or confusing. Any language that's being used in a memoir needs to be understood by the reader. There's an ongoing debate in Hawaiʻi about the use of pidgin. In both fiction and nonfiction, many writers revert to standard English for the ease of the reader, interjecting special language or dialect at special times. Others feel strongly that writing in pidgin or dialect keeps the writing authentic.

"When you tell someone's story using their own words," Pamela Varma Brown says, "they come alive on the page. Capture the flavor of how someone speaks so your readers feel like they actually know the person whose story you are telling." Still, she advises, the goal is to make sure the reader understands what is being said. "Balance how much slang or pidgin you incorporate and make the spelling easy for anyone to read and understand." She also reminds writers that even people who speak pidgin are used to reading standard English, so ultimately it is up to you how you want the language to look on the page.

Start by going with your gut. If it doesn't feel right to cast a conversation with your neighbor in perfect English when he only speaks pidgin, go ahead and try to write it in pidgin, making sure to keep it consistent and ensure that the words spoken are still understood by the reader. If that doesn't work, consider keeping the conversation in a narrative form instead of dialogue or breaking out part of the conversation in dialogue and keeping some in narrative form.

"I no trust dem guys, dey no da kine." (We hear how he sounds but may not understand what he's saying.)

vs.

"I don't trust those guys, they have ulterior motives." (Sounds too formal and stilted.)

vs.

My neighbor said he never trusted the developers because he knew they had ulterior motives. (Works, but flat.)

vs.

My neighbor was convinced the developers had ulterior motives. "I no trust dem guys," he told me. (We "hear" him and also understand the intention behind his words.)

One final note on language. Sometimes what is unsaid is just as powerful as what is said.

Example:

"What happened to Tūtū in Honolulu?"
Everyone froze around the table. Finally my mother tapped her chopsticks against my bowl but refused to look me in the eye. "Eat your rice," she said quietly.
We never spoke about it again.

FIRST DRAFTS

Here's the thing about first drafts.

You need one.

The idea of a memoir will only take you so far. You actually need to write it down, to get it from your head (and maybe your heart?) and onto the page.

> *"So write, just pick up your pen and write. You have a story to tell, don't worry about grammar or spelling, this is your first rough draft, just put it down on paper."*
> **FRANCES KAKUGAWA**

As obvious as this may seem, it is also the most difficult step. The temptation to stop, to edit, to throw it away and start again may plague you as you try to reach the end.

But here's the things about first drafts. They're exactly that: *first.* Some people call them rough drafts because they're exactly that as well: *rough.* They're not supposed to be perfect. They're not supposed to work right out the gate. What they are supposed to be is as much as you can get down about the thing you want to write about. Right now that is your only job. Get it down.

Mark Panek advises writers to get it done sooner rather than later: "The goal should always be to write the first draft of each chapter as quickly as possible, understanding that it will be revised again and again. No one writes well when they're jammed up. But if you keep in mind that you've never read anything in a book that hasn't been revised multiple times to look as good as it does, it's much easier to let it rip in that first draft."

Victoria Kneubuhl stresses the difference between the creative process and the revision process: "Try, as much as possible, to avoid editing yourself when you are working on the first draft. You need to give your imagination and your voice a free space. Writing creatively and editing are two different functions."

Once you have a first draft, the magic begins. The crafting, the possibilities. When you have a draft, you can go places. With a draft, you can see what works and what doesn't. A finished first draft, however terrible or awful or awkward or embarrassing, is an amazing thing. *Now* you can worry about fixing those grammatical mistakes, double checking a fact, deleting or revising a section you've been thinking about. You don't want to spend time doing this in the beginning, because there's a chance you may end up deleting it later on, and all that extra editing was for naught. It's too early in the process to be refining, because you still don't understand what you have. Not yet. You'll know what you have when you're holding that finished first draft in your hands.

First drafts are a sign that you are ready for more. So get yourself writing, and don't stop until you've written all there is to be written about your story. You'll feel it. Even if the ending isn't exactly right, you'll know when you are done or near done.

And from there you can go anywhere.

HŌ'IKE HO'OPŌKOLE: CHAPTER SUMMARY

✓ A well-written memoir is the result of a set of deliberate choices (made by you) about what to share and how to share it.

✓ Memoirs are often referred to as creative nonfiction, which means that while it's based on a true story, it's presented as a story in the same way fiction is.

✓ How a character is portrayed and introduced to a reader is paramount, especially if that character is you.

✓ Plots are the story behind the story.

✓ Story arc is the map that leads the way.

✓ Themes inform the reader what your memoir is about so they know what to expect.

✓ Details are the cream of a story and enrich your memoir.

✓ Show, don't tell. Let the reader experience the story so they become a part of the story.

✓ Dialogue helps move the story forward and imparts additional information to the reader.

✓ Every memoirist needs a first draft, however imperfect, awkward, embarrassing or terrible the draft may be. One you have a first draft, the fun begins.

CHAPTER FOUR
PERMISSION

'Ae

You have finally begun to write. It feels good, even fun, to recall the details of your past and bring them to the page. Some things you remembered easily, and other things slipped in while you were writing. Small surprises, an ingot of gold here and there. The writing is flowing. It's good.

And then an old face looms up, holding up a forbidding hand.

STOP.

You can't write about that. We don't hang our dirty laundry for other people to see. This is a family secret. This is not what happened. You will embarrass and bring shame on this family. Your memory is wrong. You are wrong. We never could trust you. No one will believe you. We will be angry. We will no longer speak to you. We will deny everything. We will sue.

STOP STOP STOP.

You're frozen with fear and trepidation. What do you do?

QUIET COURAGE

Writing about our lives involves courage. Even if you don't have any aspirations to publish your work, it takes courage to write down the details of a past event that may have been difficult or shrouded in secrecy. Keeping the silence sometimes means not acknowledging it at all. When you put it down in black and white, you've betrayed that unspoken understanding.

In writing your memoir or story, you are writing *your* truth. It is not your job to get into anybody else's head or even figure out their motivations. In writing about other people, they are only there in the context of your life. Writing for revenge or with the intent to embarrass, humiliate or make someone accountable for something they did in the past is fraught with problems. Don't go there. Write only about these people as much as you need to. You are not telling their story, you are telling yours. They can write their own memoirs if they have something to say.

> *"Be honest. Once you begin to censor your work because you're afraid of what others will say, you will lose the power of writing. Memoirs are not all nice and pretty. Memoirs are honest stories of real people who lived or are living."*
> **FRANCES KAKUGAWA**

In Hawaiian, the word *kuleana* means ownership and responsibility. We have a responsibility to care for one another, just as we need to take responsibility for ourselves and our own actions. Does this mean covering up a lie or shameful act? Does this mean keeping the family peace by not mentioning an encounter that changed your life? Only you can answer that. Remember: Just because it happened doesn't mean you have to write about it. That's right. A memoir does not have to include everything *just because it happened*. It's not about right and wrong.

Cedric Yamanaka counsels honesty. "Create something as close to the truth as possible," he says. Write about it because it's relevant to your story. Write about it because if you don't, who you are and why you've made the choices you have make no sense. Write about it because it affected you, possibly even changed your life. Write about it because you want to remember. Write about it because keeping it inside consumes you. Write about it so you can move on.

We have an authority to speak honestly about how we feel and how something affected us. Secrets have rarely served anyone—we all know this. To have respect for yourself and the people around you, you have to be willing to look at the truth of your life and speak to it. Kuleana is not about good manners or making (much less keeping) other people happy. It's about a deeper, higher truth. It requires quiet courage.

SAVING FACE: WHEN PERSONAL IS NO LONGER PRIVATE

Many of us are familiar with the term "save face" or "saving face." In Asian cultures, this refers to actions that cover up mistakes to maintain a reputation or standing in society. It's the reason why so much family history (including medical history) is covered up and lost. The more shameful, the higher the stakes. Making parents or the family "lose face" may result in being disinherited or even expelled from the family. Being gay, abandoning a successful career, forsaking family responsibilities or contracting a debilitating disease are all grounds for losing face. Talking back or speaking up might earn you a slap across the face or silent treatment that lasts a lifetime.

Because saving face is so ingrained in Asian cultures and has become an integral part of local Hawai'i culture, it is often difficult to write about our parents or grandparents. Again, it is not the job of the memoirist to make others "face up" to the past. Your job is to determine what it meant for you.

Writing memoir means taking something that was once private and laying it out for the world to see. Because we want the reader to connect with us (the protagonist and hero of our memoir), we have to watch that we don't compromise our writing to "save face" as well. There's a reason we wash up, brush our teeth, put on deodorant and dress nicely before we leave the house. Very few of us just roll out of bed and go. We want to look our best and influence others into liking us (versus not liking us). We know it's superficial (It shouldn't really make a difference if we're wearing makeup or not, right?), and yet we still continue to do it.

> *"Beyond legal concerns are the real and sometimes life-altering consequences of writing something true that harms or offends someone you've written about."*
> **MARK PANEK**

In writing the memoir, we have to be willing to "lose face" or "make A" (another local term) if that is what happened. If you did something you are not proud of but it impacted your life, write about it. We are just as imperfect as you, and we hope to learn from our mistakes as well. Generations of people "saving face" have caused more distress and unhappiness than peace. Be willing to drop the charade altogether. It will set you free.

PERMISSION VS. COURTESY

If someone appears in your memoir, you have the option of sharing your work with them. If you choose to do this, it is a courtesy, a way to allow others to respond especially if the time was long ago and you are sensitive as to how it may affect them. The danger in sharing your work, of course, is the expectation that you might change or remove something if asked to. The pressure is now on, and depending on the nature of your relationship, you may or may not be able to stand by your work. Before showing your work to someone who appears in your memoir, ask yourself first *why* you are showing it to them.

It's tricky, because some of us share not for courtesy or even corroboration ("Was it really raining that day?") but for approval. We want the people we write about to be okay with what we've done. We want their permission to write or publish what we have written. We might even be secretly hoping that they'll tell us they liked what we wrote, that we've somehow gained or maintained their respect for us. This slippery slope does not promise a comfortable ride down.

Some memoirists will leave out whole incidents in the interest of maintaining the relationship. The question to ask yourself is: *Do you need it?* Writing the memoir is an ongoing process of choosing what to include and what to exclude. This decision should be based on the story you wish to share that reveals more of who you are and who you've become.

> *"Before deciding whether to write about the dark side of an experience, or of another person, reflect whether the event is accurate and relevant to telling your story. If it is not, don't use it."*
> **BEN CAYETANO**

If and when you do show it to someone to ensure the details and amount of revelation are accurate, be prepared for them to have second thoughts, change their mind or withdraw their consent altogether. If this happens, come up with a Plan B. Because your memoir is about you, your story should not hinge on someone else's details. There are other ways to write about an event or person that do not compromise personal information. Getting too specific with other people's sensitive material may be appropriate for their memoir, but not yours.

One last thing to remember: You don't need permission from others to write your own story, but make sure you're writing your story and not someone else's (see the Appendices for other life-writing forms). The purpose of the memoir is to share your emotional journey, so the extent to which you include other people's lives or details needs to be carefully considered. Make sure that it is relevant to the point you are trying to make and decide how much you need to reveal.

HO'Ā'O: TRY THIS

I Can't Write About That
Make a quick list of five things you don't want to write about or feel you shouldn't write about. Then take the first item on that list and write for ten minutes about the worst thing that could happen if you wrote about it. It won't be easy. (That's why you didn't want to write about it in the first place, right?) But if you want to write a memoir and write it well, you want to free up any stuck places. So start by calling those stuck places by name and poking around a little bit. You still don't need to write about them, but we want to remove the reluctance or even dread that surrounds it, to lessen your immediate negative response so you can consider it—and anything else you might encounter on this writing path—and its possible role in your story. When you are finished, feel free to keep, shred, burn or delete the document—it doesn't matter. Your work here is done.

TALKING STINK: LIBEL, COPYRIGHT INFRINGEMENT AND OTHER LEGAL RISKS

If we're writing our truth based on our experiences and memory, does that mean we're off the hook for legal risks or exposure?

One of the greatest fears of any memoirist is getting into trouble—legal trouble—as a result of something they've written. In particular they worry about the threat of a lawsuit, which is costly both financially and emotionally. It seems easier to not write anything that might risk exposure, and indeed many people give up writing their memoirs for this very reason.

"Understand that even in memoir, the moment you begin writing about other people, you are writing biography and thus entering a minefield of legal and ethical concerns," says Mark Panek. "You can cause harm and you can be sued, even if what you say is true."

There are a few things to consider here. First, writing about it is not the same thing as publishing it. Until you have a finished manuscript, until you have polished every chapter, until you have gone through the work of ensuring that what you've put in (or taken out) serves the greater good of the story, you don't have to worry about this. You are just writing. That's all. People wouldn't keep journals if they were worried about being sued for their personal writing that's kept safe in their bedside table. We all know that it's difficult, if not impossible, to write if we are worried about potential consequences.

Second, you want to make sure you are not mentioning specific people or events to hold them accountable or to exact a literary form of revenge. This may sound silly, but it's not. There is a purity with the memoir form in that it emerges from you—it is a form of self-expression. Don't taint it by mudslinging or subtle insinuations. Readers don't like that nor do they want to get dragged in to any unresolved personal drama. Remember that memoir is about

> *"Life-writing can and does cause harm, and determining whether or not you're willing to do that should be part of the writing process."*
> **CRAIG HOWES**

what you have learned, not what you are still going through. Make sure you are bringing in those moments that offer reflection, not distress or anger.

Third, if you do choose to include details about another person and mention them by name, be sure to keep track of any emails that can become part of your research and verification process. More complicated issues or events may require a legal release of some kind—if this is the case, you'll want to consult a lawyer. Most people will not find themselves in this situation, so don't panic. But if it involves celebrities, minors, contracts, lawsuits or anything that smells complicated or complex, consider seeking legal advice.

When you're ready to foray into the world of publication, either self-publication or through a traditional publisher, is when you want to explore these issues. Even if you plan to share your work on a public forum (such as a blog or writing website), you will want to educate yourself on what legal risks you may face. Does every memoirist need to run their manuscript through an attorney? Of course not. Writing about real people, dead or alive, is not illegal—if it was, newspapers, magazines and news channels wouldn't exist. It's *how* you write about them that matters.

The best way to determine whether or not you need legal help is to educate yourself first on what areas of the law may affect you and then look at your memoir to see if they apply. Following are some common legal terms you may encounter that can be associated with memoir writing.

Libel is when you write something false about someone that damages that person's reputation. Truth is an absolute defense to such a claim. So, if you must write something negative about someone, make sure that what you write is the truth and be sure to keep all of the evidence (such as emails or other documents) that support what you have written.

Copyright comes into play the moment something is written, regardless of whether or not anything is filed with the U.S. Copyright Office. A work has copyright protection from the moment it is written, but this extends beyond a manuscript like your memoir to include documents like letters written by your grandparents, who technically own the copyright for those letters. The law used to hold that a person had to include a copyright notice such as a © on a work in order to have copyright protection. However, under current law, such a notice is not required for any work first published after March 1, 1989. As a result, unless you are absolutely certain that a work was published without a copyright notice before that date, you must assume that someone owns the copyright on all writings (including poems and song lyrics), photographs, paintings and other works (whether you see them in person, on the Internet or anywhere else) and that you cannot use them without getting the copyright owner's consent.

There are certain limited circumstances in which someone else's copyrighted work may be used without their permission. Such circumstances, referred to as *fair use*, permit use of someone else's work for purposes such as criticism, comment, news reporting, scholarship or research. To determine whether or not a particular usage is fair use, the courts consider the following factors:

∗ The purpose and character of the use, including whether such use is of a commercial nature or is for nonprofit educational purposes
∗ The nature of the copyrighted work
∗ The amount and substantiality of the portion used in relation to the copyrighted work as a whole
∗ The effect of the use upon the potential market for, or value of, the copyrighted work

Even if your memoir will be produced in a very small quantity and distributed only to family and friends, it is subject to copyright laws. If you use someone else's work without permission for a memoir that you produce only for yourself, it is still technically an infringement. Consider the thousands of cases brought by recording industry companies against individuals who downloaded music for their own use. Of course, if you copy a photograph or portions of some literary work and show it to only a few people, it's also unlikely that the copyright owner will ever find out about it, but you should at least be aware of the possible legal ramifications.

There are places to look to determine copyright ownership, including the U.S. Copyright Office's searchable database and the ASCAP and BMI websites for music copyrights (song lyrics). There are also commercial sites available that will perform searches for you. But keep in mind that such searches now serve only as a basis to determine who owns the copyright and, therefore, as a means of identifying who you should approach to get permission to use. What's more, they are useless in determining whether anyone owns a copyright in a work first published after March 1, 1989.

Some general rules on copyright duration: Works published with a copyright notice before January 1, 1978 are subject to an initial term of twenty-eight years plus a renewal term of sixty-seven years for a total of ninety-five years. For works created on or after January 1, 1978, the copyright is in effect for the life of the author plus seventy years after the author's death—and, in the case of an anonymous work, a pseudonymous work or a work made for hire, for a term of ninety-five years from the year of first publication or 120 years from the year of its creation, whichever expires first. The same holds true for works existing but not published or copyrighted on January 1, 1978. There are a number of other considerations as to whether a copyright is still in effect, or whether or not a work is in the public domain, and as a result, copyright search and resolution can be a bewildering task.

Invasion of privacy can occur when you write something about someone that they don't want to be shared. Generally, people have the right to be let alone and/or free from publicity. A work may encroach upon that right if:

* It includes detailed information about a private person's sexual conduct, medical condition or educational record
* It unflatteringly portrays someone in a false manner that is highly offensive to a reasonable person
* It makes unauthorized use of a person's name, photograph, likeness, voice or endorsement to promote the sale of a commercial product or service

There are circumstances under which publishing such information does not constitute an invasion of privacy, such as when something is truly newsworthy.

If this is an area that concerns you, take some time to understand what these terms really mean. Knowledge is power and it will remove or at least alleviate the uncertainty and anxiety around your memoir. But in the meantime, don't let it stop you from writing. This is something you should concern yourself with only after you've finished writing and know for sure what you want to have published. Spending time and money on legal advice for a chapter-in-progress that you end up throwing out in the final draft is frustrating (not to mention expensive).

The good news is that there are things you can do to help protect yourself and your writing. Employ them to the extent you need to, but don't go overboard or you risk moving your memoir into the realm of fiction. Some things you can do are (and, if appropriate, acknowledge at the front of your book):

* Change names or create composite characters (two or more characters mashed into one)
* Disguise identifying characteristics or details
* Qualify controversial or questionable statements as your own
* Be as thorough as possible to verify what you can to minimize risk (Was it really the candy store or was it the crack seed store?)

Here are some final things to keep in mind when writing your memoir:

* Don't make assumptions about what another person is feeling or thinking unless they said it out loud
* Don't put words in their mouths that were not said (even if it might have felt like they said it or they implied it)
* Don't make things up or embellish to make a boring story sound more interesting or exciting
* Don't include details or facts for shock value
* Don't lie
* Don't deliberately misconstrue or mislead for storytelling purposes
* Don't write for revenge or to make someone "own" up to something
* Don't be paranoid
* Don't try to tell anyone else's story but yours

Oh, and one last thing: Write anyway.

HŌʻIKE HOʻOPŌKOLE: CHAPTER SUMMARY

✓ In writing your memoir or story, you are writing your truth.

✓ If other people disagree with what you wrote or how you felt, they can write their own memoirs.

✓ It is not the job of the memoirist to make others "face up" to the past. Your job is to determine what it meant for you.

✓ You don't need permission from others to write your own story.

✓ Educate yourself on legal risks after you've finished writing and know for sure what you want to have published.

✓ Write anyway.

CHAPTER FIVE
CHALLENGES & ROADBLOCKS

ʻĀkeʻakeʻa

Writing should be fun, but that doesn't mean it'll be easy. The writer's path is often littered with emotional debris—doubt, uncertainty, second guessing, lack of confidence. There are other challenges, too—lack of funds, lack of time, lack of space, lack of support from others. You can't do much about the things out of your control, but there is plenty you can do about the things that are in your control. How you feel, what you choose to believe and taking care of yourself physically and mentally are all ways that you can set yourself up for writing (and living) well.

Make a choice, and make it with me now. Don't hang out with negativity or negative people, be kind to yourself, remember that being able to write your story is a remarkable gift, both to you as the writer and to any future readers. If you do hit a roadblock or two, here are a few ways over, around or through.

THE DREADED WRITER'S BLOCK

Writer's block is that frustrating phenomenon that happens when you find yourself frozen, unable to write another word or hating every word you write. There are countless debates about writer's block, what it is and how to fix it.

Writer's block does not strike at random. It's not as if you wake up one morning with writer's block, like catching a cold or case of the

> *"If you find yourself getting stuck at any point, put your work aside for a few days. Sometimes things work themselves out in mysterious ways."*
> **VICTORIA KNEUBUHL**

chills. It's not because the muse has stopped favoring you or that your creative well has dried up. It's not as if you've somehow forgotten how to write, because you are probably continuing to write in other areas of your life—emails, documents for work, papers for school, grocery lists, letters to old friends. Your ability to write hasn't changed one iota—just your ability to write whatever it is you're working on.

The term "writer's block" is exactly that—a block. Something is in your way and preventing you from moving forward. The good news is that there is a reason. The bad news is you need to figure out what that reason is.

In many cases, our immediate response is to shut down. It's a survival instinct—the brain recognizes that something is about to cause discomfort or suffering and it does its best to save us from it. It doesn't understand that in this work, we're not looking to avoid or ignore things anymore. We want, in fact, to set it free.

Perhaps you hit a sensitive vein regarding the topic you're writing. It's also possible to be blocked when old fears emerge, not so much about *what* you're writing, but the process of writing itself. What if you're no good? What if you write and people laugh? What if they say you're wrong? And so on and so on.

We're also human and, unfortunately, at times a bit lazy. Can't get a scene to work? Or the writing feels flat or uninteresting? Or maybe you just plain hate what you've written and don't ever want to pick up a pen again? The thought of figuring out how to "fix" or revise a piece of writing can be frustrating or even hard. It's so much easier to just give it up, because who needs that kind of grief?

You do, that's who. Because this is your story and you care enough about what you're writing to write it honestly and write it well. Writing does not always come easily, even for the best of writers. Writing is work, especially if you are pulling up the past, and even more so if you are crafting your memoir for publication.

So what to do? One option—and the simplest—is to stop. Certainly don't beat yourself up or feel guilty that you can't write. Sitting in a chair and staring at a blank page for hours isn't productive either. Stopping can take one of two forms: a full-on break, where you shelve your work and turn your attention elsewhere, or a stop from the crazy thoughts whirling around in your head that are undermining you. Either way will help you interrupt a pattern that's not productive and maybe even bordering on punishing. The first way will give your work a chance to settle and when you return to it with fresh eyes, whatever the problem was may have presented a solution or no longer feels troublesome.

For others, the second way is called for; the best way out is through. This method—stopping any defeating thoughts—helps you to learn how to get out of your own way, if that's the problem. Writing, like all things, improves with practice. The longer you are away from it, well, the longer you are away from it. If you want to write, you need to be writing. It's the best way I know to improve your craft and reach your goal of finishing your memoir and becoming a better writer. You literally and figuratively need to write your way through it, like an ox pulling a plow through stubborn earth.

One thing that may help is learning to shift your attention. If you are stuck on a particular story or memory, try writing about a related event even though it may have little bearing on your story (Or so you think!). For example, if you are trying to write about the first time you went fishing with your grandfather off the Hilo Pier, but can't seem to get the two of you out of the truck where a heavy conversation ensued about how he was going to leave your eighty-year-old grandmother, skip ahead to lunch. What did you eat? Did you eat? What did you talk about? Skip ahead to the drive home. What did you catch? How did you say goodbye? If that feels too hard, skip ahead to the next day, even if neither your grandfather or grandmother were a part of it. How did you feel when you woke up? What did you do? Did you think about the day before at all? How did you feel?

The point here is to get you out of the muck and moving again. It's fine to delve deeper into *why* you seem unable to write, but see if you can do it while you're writing, too. If writing through it proves too difficult, just find something else less sticky to write about, and put that story on the shelf or up for discussion with a friend, writing mentor or therapist. There are plenty of stories from your life to write about—you could easily be writing multiple memoirs for a lifetime if that's your desire. So if the one you're working one is stubborn and not letting you pass, don't fight it. Just sidestep it for now and keep going. When you're ready, you can come back to it, or you may find something better has shown up.

Christine Thomas says, "I believe writer's block actually means you have too many ideas (not none) and just aren't able to focus on one." She recommends timed freewrites where the pen never leaves the page. If you're stuck, write "I don't know what to write" until the ideas begin to flow. "They will," she says, "and don't let that internal critic prevent them from making it to the page. Step away, and then with fresh eyes determine the idea or ideas that bring you back to writing again. I'm always surprised at what I find after this exercise, and have learned it's a great way to get started, too."

OVERWHELMED

Feeling overwhelmed is a lousy feeling. It's not about being stuck or unable to write (though you may be experiencing that as well). It can be as simple as too many things going on at once. We all know what that feels like.

Writing projects can quickly take on that feeling. We wake up one morning and wonder what we've gotten ourselves into with no idea how to get out. We can't just throw these stories away, and yet the thought of working any more feels impossible.

Maybe it's not the demands of writing, but the demands of life. Your daily routine doesn't leave room to create—how could it? Something has to go, and seeing how you can't get rid of your kids or your spouse or your job or those dirty dishes or the busted car, abandoning your memoir project seems like the only option.

It's not. It's really not, and I'll tell you why.

Writing is an inside-out job. We were born to create. We all have different gifts and desires and dreams, but if writing is one of yours, don't give it up. You can find a way to make it a part of your day even if it means revising your writing goals. You can write a first draft of a memoir in ten minutes a day and have something to show for it a year later. *You* made this. You, and possibly others (family members, readers, the world at large), will have this thing, this memoir, this wonderful book.

There will always be dirty dishes. There will always be grumpy neighbors. There will always be demanding family members.

If you are feeling overwhelmed, find help. You're a creative person, so find a creative solution to your problems. If something you've tried hasn't worked, try something else. Remind yourself of what's important here: you. Writing will help keep you connected to that authentic part of you that can do anything. So you've gotten a little distracted—who hasn't? They key is to steer your ship back in the right direction. You are the captain of your life, after all. Even if you can't change all the external demands of your life right away, you can change the way you feel about them and how much you're willing to allow those feelings to affect you. And you've got a great first mate that's available to help you any time, all the time.

> *"Write in any form that you like; poems, stories or just fragments like a shopping list. Whatever makes you comfortable, whatever comes to mind...just get your words down on paper."*
> **FRANCES KAKUGAWA**

Writing.

If you can't find help in life, find help in writing. Look for a writing partner or a writing mentor. Look for resources online. Join a writer's group or write to your favorite memoirist or author. Read. Write. Journal every morning, do timed writing exercises, take a writing workshop or class. Writing will help loosen up the tight spots and help put things into perspective. It'll deflate that feeling of being overwhelmed and, worst of all, helpless. Every little bit helps, and it can make a big difference.

And once you've gotten through with it, guess what? You can write about it and help others who may one day be exactly where you once were.

DOUBT

Doubt is tricky and insidious. It looks benign, a simple question mark, but while you're observing its somewhat subdued nature, it's busy unraveling your confidence down below.

Doubt is deep stuff because it presents the possibility that we are somehow not good enough. It poses everything as a question.

"Are you sure you can do this? I mean, no offense, but you barely passed English class in high school, you know?"

Doubt plants the thought then takes off, leaving us to ruminate and fret. Doubt loves to stir the pot but only when we're not looking. Doubt peeks over our shoulder and lets out a small gasp when it sees what we're writing.

"You're writing about that? What if you get in trouble?"

Doubt doesn't have friends and couldn't care less if the critic or your mother has something good or bad to say—doubt can cast a shadow on any comment.

Doubt will play with you if you let it. *Don't let it.* Don't indulge it, don't listen politely, don't argue with it. Doubt has been at this a long time and knows how to play this game. You can't convince it otherwise.

So if you're writing and doubts start to surface—"Should I be writing about this? Maybe I need to take a class or hire someone else to write this instead?"—you're going to have to be rude and just ignore it. That's the only way to work with doubt. It'll keep knocking on your door trying to sell you something and it won't take anything less than a "NO!" to get it to go away. Even then, it still may knock again. Best you just don't answer the door when you know doubt's there.

Here are a few key words that let you know doubt might be lurking about:

* should
* supposed to
* but what if
* not good enough
* not ready
* it's not a good time
* someone else can do a better job
* who would want to read this

If you have thoughts or conversations that include these words, be vigilant. Doubt is playing you, you can be sure of it. It doesn't matter if you're a novice writer or a successfully published author—doubt doesn't play favorites.

"I wish someone had told me how much self-confidence was required of a writer on a daily basis," Victoria Kneubuhl observes. "I have done lots of other things for way more money that didn't require half of the skill or effort that writing requires. I wish someone had told me how restless and dissatisfied I would always be with my work, how there would be no such thing as resting on any laurels, and how I would only feel as good as the last sentence I had written. I wish someone had told me that I would always be reaching for something that was just a little beyond my grasp. I wish someone had told me that once I started writing, I would never be able to stop."

> *"There are times when you have to be bold, face down your demons and find out who you really are as a writer."*
> **STUART HOLMES COLEMAN**

HOʻĀʻO: TRY THIS

Honor Roll

First, write down a list of ten things you have done or accomplished in your life, especially if it's something where you stood out from other people. Even if other people placed more value on it than you did, write it down. Even if it happened in the third grade, write it down. All the better if it was something you were proud of or if it made you realize your own strength and abilities. Ten may sound like a lot, but it's not. If you can't come up with ten, consider asking a friend or someone close to you to name one or two things you've done in your life that they thought were pretty cool or impressive. Then write a short sentence or paragraph explaining why the event was so significant. Keep it somewhere near your writing area to remind you of what you have already done in your life—some of these moments may even find their way into your memoir.

HO'Ā'O: TRY THIS

The Values List

The values list is a great way to remind yourself of who you are and what matters to you. Doubt flounders in the face of personal values. Following is a list of key Hawaiian values. Circle the top ten values that represent or resonate closely to you. Once you have your ten, put them in order of priority. You do not have to share this list or show it to anyone. Keep this list nearby to help you in moments of stress or doubt. In writing, we never want to forget who we are or what matters most, so having a list like this helps us remember).

alaka'i (leadership)

aloha (unconditional love and respect)

ha'aha'a (humility, modesty)

hau'oli (happy)

ho'āmana (empowerment)

ho'ohana (to work with intent and purpose)

ho'ohānai (to nurture)

ho'okipa (hospitality, to entertain)

ho'olauna (friendliness)

ho'omanawanui (patience, perseverance)

ho'omau (to continue, perpetuate, steadfast)

huikala (forgiveness)

ikaika (strength)

ka lā hiki ola (optimism)

koa (courage, bravery)

kūlia i ka nu'u (achievement, accomplishment)

kūha'o (independence)

kuleana (responsibility)

kūpono (honesty, fairness)

le'ale'a (fun)

lōkahi (harmony collaboration, unity)

lokomaika'i (generosity, benevolence)

mahalo (appreciation, thankfulness)

mākaukau (preparedness)

mālama (caring, stewardship)

mana'o'i'o (faith, confidence, belief)

mana'olana (hope)

menemene (compassion)

na'auao (knowledge, intelligence)

nani (beauty)

'ohana (family)

ohohia (enthusiasm)

'oia'i'o (truth)

ola (health, well being)

'olu'olu (gracious, courteous, kindness)

pa'ahana (diligent, hardworking)

po'okela (to constantly seek improvement, to excel)

pono (correctness, fairness, goodness, morality)

wiwo'ole (bravery, courage, fearless)

HO'A'O: TRY THIS

A Valuable Memoir

In this exercise, write a personal essay or memoir for each of your ten values, drawing on experiences from your life to demonstrate why each value is significant to you. Working back from ten to one, with one being your most important value, you'll end up with ten different personal essays. This memoir is a succinct yet powerful way to share who you are with others.

THE CRITIC

The critic needs no introduction. The critic is the voice inside of us that doesn't question if we're good enough, it tells us we're not good enough. There is no pleasing the critic, even when you do something well or right. "That wouldn't be half bad if you hadn't written it *that* way," or "Wow, I thought it was going to turn out better than that. Guess not." The critic likes to harp on missed deadlines, wrong story turns,

> *"Poke at assumptions, especially the ones inside your head."*
> **BETH-ANN KOZLOVICH**

wasted time. "That was a dumb move," it'll say, or "I'm embarrassed for you, even if you don't have the good sense to be." Nothing is ever good enough for the internal critic. The only way to beat the internal critic is to ignore it.

In addition to the internal critic, there are external ones as well. They may take the form of fellow authors, readers, reviewers, editors, agents, publishers. Friends and families usually provide their fair share of critics as well.

It's hard to discern what kind of criticism is helpful, as most of it's not. Really. As a writer, you'll need to learn to distinguish comments that are meant to be helpful and can strengthen your writing from those meant to distract or detract from it. If you start taking the criticism personally, take a step back. The only feedback you are interested in has to do with your work, and all work has room for improvement. Look at the feedback in the spirit it was given and run it through your own filter. Is what is being said helpful in any way? Is it worth trying on for size?

Don't set yourself up for discouragement by asking for feedback from people who aren't in a position to give it. If your memoir isn't the kind of book they would normally read, don't put them on the spot by asking them to take a look. Don't secretly hope for approval. Ask only if you are looking for constructive feedback on your work and make sure you're asking people who know how to give it.

FINISHING

There are writers who get close to the finish line but never cross it. They may spend weeks, months, even years of their life working on their memoir, then stop when the end is in sight. Alternatively, they may drag out the last quarter of the book, citing a need for more research, a snag in the writing, a possible shift in focus. It doesn't matter if this happens with the first draft or the twentieth.

There's something about endings that throw us all into a tailspin. After all that work, it's finally over. We may have mixed feelings about this—relief, disappointment, fear. What do we do next? If you've poured yourself into your work, nearing the end can be almost anticlimactic. Some people are addicted to beginnings—the anticipation and excitement of what's to come is enough to kickstart them into writing.

> *"Sit down and make yourself do it because it is one of the greatest gifts you can bequeath to your family. Just think: Your grandchildren's grandchildren will know all that you know right now about who their ancestors were, where they came from, how their family used to live and what you hope for them."*
> **LESLIE LANG**

So how do you cross that finish line? By doing what you've been doing all along—writing one word at a time, one page at a time, until you reach the end. Don't change course and suddenly decide you should rewrite the whole thing or need to do more research. Finish first. Remember: A completed draft can go places, but a partially-finished manuscript will fester, tormenting you. Even if you feel you've written a terrible first draft, you now have something you can work with. First drafts, no matter how awful, are good. It's difficult to revise an incomplete manuscript because you don't know where it's going—you think you do, but the truth is until you type THE END (literally or figuratively), you don't really know what you have.

So cross that finish line. We'll be on the other side, cheering you on.

HŌʻIKE HOʻOPŌKOLE: CHAPTER SUMMARY

✔ Writing does not always come easily, even for the best of writers.

✔ Writing is an inside-out job.

✔ You're a creative person—find a creative solution to your problems.

✔ Doubt will play with you if you let it. Don't let it.

✔ The only way to beat the internal critic is to ignore it.

✔ Don't set yourself up for disappointment by asking for feedback from people who aren't in a position to give you helpful feedback.

✔ Keep writing one word at a time, one page at a time, until you reach the end.

✔ Even if you feel you've written a terrible first draft, you now have something you can work with.

CHAPTER SIX
REVISING

Hoʻoponopono Hou

Finishing a manuscript is a powerful thing. If you haven't already, you should be celebrating (or sleeping, for those of you who tossed and turned at night during the writing process). It's a huge—really huge—accomplishment.

So now what? You're done, right? The hard work is over and now you can run the spell check on your computer or have your neighbor take one last look then send it to a printer or find a publisher. Right?

Well, no. Good writing involves revisions and that's where you are now. When you hear people talk about the craft of writing, this is where that happens. Very few authors are able to write a first draft that doesn't require even a little tweaking, and most drafts require a lot. Even those of us who edit as we go, red pen and all, know that we'll need to go back once the book is finished and go through everything again.

WHY REVISE? FROM GOOD TO GREAT

Up until now you've had your writer hat on. Now you're putting your editor hat on. Later, when you begin to explore ways to get your work out into the world, you'll put your marketing and business hat on. Making this deliberate shift also triggers another part of your brain to turn on and get ready to buckle down. Believe it or not, a lot of the basic editing skills you'll need are already in your head. Really.

You know how to edit because you read. Newspapers, books, magazines, websites, advertisements, birthday cards. You went to school for enough years to know how to put a sentence together, even if you couldn't begin to explain it to

> *"Learn to love rewriting, because rewriting is where you can turn lead into gold."*
> **VICTORIA KNEUBUHL**

another person. You know what a dictionary is, you know what a thesaurus is. You know—based on your own circle of friends, families, coworkers and neighbors—who can help you if you need help.

When you edit your work, you will go through several stages of revisions, sometimes in order, sometimes out of order and sometimes simultaneously. Approach this work with a plan, and understand that you may be reading through your memoir several times in order to examine different things.

The power of a first draft is not unlike preparing a great meal. At this stage you have all the ingredients out on the kitchen counter. What comes next—prepping what you have, determining the right quantities, the proper order in which to add them to the recipe, how long to cook it for so everything is timed perfectly—is the work of revision.

Editing may feel like drudgery for a lot of people, but experienced writers know that this is where the fun begins. Knowing what you're looking for takes away the guesswork and uncertainty. Writing is largely a creative process—but so is editing. You'll make choices that will help shape your memoir so that it's not merely good, but great.

EDITING

At this stage some people will opt to hire someone to do the editorial work of their manuscript (read more about this in the Hired Help section in Chapter Seven, *Feedback and Sharing*). I'm a big believer in learning how to be your own best editor first, for the simple reason that (1) it's cheaper and (2) all writers need to know how to cast a careful eye over their manuscript. This is a skill that you can learn and should learn, especially if you have more than one book inside of you.

> *"Editing takes time, but that's where the magic happens, where your story becomes powerful."*
> **PAMELA VARMA BROWN**

I know plenty of people who spent money on editors and were unhappy with the work or ended up having to do it themselves in the end anyway. If using someone to help with the editing of your manuscript is something you prefer to do, by all means go for it, but you'll still need to know enough to determine if they've done a good job. Only after you've undertaken several revisions of your own should you look to hire an outside editor.

Frances Kakugawa reminds us that editing is not personal. "Editors do not edit writers, only their writing," she says. So bear this in mind when someone looks over your carefully chosen words and recommends all manner of changes.

There are two kinds of editing in this work: copy editing and content editing. Copy editing looks at sentence structure, spelling errors, grammatical errors, inconsistencies, overuse or repetitiveness of certain word. Content editing looks at story flow, at how well the writing engages the reader, where it struggles, what's confusing, the strengths and weaknesses of the work. Content editing is subjective, meaning that everyone may have a different view about what works and what doesn't, and can sometimes result in so many changes that the finished book looks nothing like the first draft. The bottom line is this: (1) did you get your point across (or did you say/show what you wanted to), and (2) does the reader want to keep turning the page?

Remember, we have our editor hat on. Our goal is to make the memoir stronger, better, more readable, more compelling. Look at your work through the eyes of a reader who doesn't know you at all but would be drawn to a story like yours. Those readers tend to look for the story first—they aren't attached to you in any personal way, so they don't feel obligated to like your book if it doesn't capture their interest.

One more thing: Sometimes the revision process can take as long as the writing itself. It depends on many factors, including your own available time and commitment, but also your ability to approach this work objectively. You could be an excellent editor for your friends but a terrible self-editor. You may feel too close to the work, or even sick of it. If you need a short break between writing and editing, take it, but don't be gone for too long. The time will come when you'll want to let the book rest and breathe—it's actually just around the corner—but for now you want to keep going.

HO'Ā'O: TRY THIS

Your Memoir at a Glance

If you don't have a table of contents, make one, even if you don't plan to include it in the final draft of your memoir. List every chapter (including prologues and epilogues) and provide a one-line summary of each.

HO'Ā'O: TRY THIS

Index Cards

If staring at a stack of pages is overwhelming, try reducing the scale. Take a stack of index cards. Each card represents one chapter (introductions, prologues, epilogues also get their own card). On each card, write down the three to five key points or events of that chapter. Also write down your own goal for that chapter—why did you write it or include it? What did you want the reader to learn or know? Once this is done, spread the cards out on the floor or a bulletin board in order. There. You now have a snapshot of your entire book. Do your key points achieve your goals?

HO'Ā'O: TRY THIS

First Lines

Frances Kakugawa reminds us that the "first few sentences that begin our story are clues to what our book is about." First lines are what draw readers in. On a piece of paper, list each chapter and the opening line of each chapter. Is your first line powerful, provocative or funny? Does it give us a sense of what's to come? Does it pull you in?

FACT CHECKING

A critical component of any life story is verifying and confirming names, dates, places and times. It's important that you consider this step, especially if the memory you are recounting is detailed or involves other people or significant events. Remember that readers are trusting you to have done the hard work of not only perusing and polishing your memories, but that the memories are accurate and true. In writing the memoir we are capturing the emotional journey, but the factual path runs alongside it. You need to be responsible for both.

Any editor or publisher you may work with will expect that any verification of facts has been done. They rarely, if ever, take on this responsibility—it is always the author's domain. Don't be surprised if you're asked to sign a contract stating this, and that you assume full responsibility (legal and otherwise) for what is written and published. This is not a shared burden—it is yours entirely.

This is not meant to scare you, but to prepare you. It's important to bear in mind that many of your memories will not call for a high level of fact checking, if at all. Writing about a walk down a beach and realizing you want to change your life is quite different from writing about a walk down a beach when you heard a cry for help and tore off into the water to save someone who later came to your house to thank you with a *ti* leaf plant you still have in your front yard (Whew!). Regardless of whether or not you mention that person by name, you will most likely be sharing the name of the beach and the general time frame in which it happened (in the summer of 1971 or June 21, 1971; morning or afternoon; etc.). Especially if the event was a few years back, you will want to make sure you got your dates right. You could keep it general and not mention this person's name at all, but a big event like that will still ask that you offer some evidence of accuracy. If you do choose to mention the person's name, you may need to get their permission unless it already appears in some other form of verified public domain, such as a newspaper.

> *"Truth is often a moving target."*
> **BETH-ANN KOZLOVICH**

The memoir is an intimate piece of writing, but what is revealed should be your story, not someone else's. If your memoir is populated by other people, always ask yourself why someone is in your story and how relevant their details are to your memoir. You'll save yourself quite a bit of headache (and possibly heartache) if you ask yourself these key questions now rather than later.

HOʻĀʻO: TRY THIS

Verify This
Go through your memoir and highlight names, dates and events that need or might need fact verification. Then compile a list and rate them 1, 2 or 3 with 1 being "needs to verify" and 3 being "no need to verify." Any items rated a 2 means you're not sure, which means it becomes a 1.

When you begin verifying your 1's, make a note about how you verified it. Save this list to share with your editor or publisher later—it'll be a helpful resource for all of you.

YOUR EDITING CHECKLIST

✳ **PROOFREADING:** Start with a clean read of your memoir. Don't take notes, try not to mark anything up. Just read. If you have an e-reader, many of them have features that allow you to read your document just like you would a book. Things to keep in mind while you're doing this first read:

❑ Did I say what I wanted to say? Is it clear? Is it awkward? Does it flow?
❑ Is my voice and tone (or the narrator's) clear and consistent?
❑ How do I feel at the end?

✳ **REORGANIZING:** Subsequent reads will look at how the book is put together and what works and what doesn't. Ask yourself:

❑ Is there a better order to present this story or stories?
❑ Can I restructure the narrative in any way to make it a better book?

✳ **REWRITING:** Reading your memoir aloud from start to finish is imperative. If you haven't done it already, now is the time to do so. A combination of reading each word, paragraph and page aloud as well as seeing how it looks printed out will better inform you of what's working and what's not. You can then consider the following:

❑ Is there a better way to express/describe this?
❑ Can I trim? Expand? Is anything missing?
❑ Does everything work? Does the book pull readers in from the first page?
❑ Is everyone in the book necessary to the story?
❑ Is there anyone missing from the book?
❑ Does the point of view and narrative voice work?
❑ Do I need more/less dialogue?
❑ Where do things slow down or speed up?
❑ Did I overwrite or over explain? Or vice versa?
❑ What parts are confusing?
❑ Is it clear what this memoir is about?
❑ Does the book have a strong or satisfying ending to the reader?
❑ Is it clear why a reader would pick up my memoir and keep reading? (This includes family members. It would be a shame to write your memoirs for your grandchildren but they don't read it because it's hard to stay engaged.)

✳ **FACT CHECKING/VERIFYING:** The next read can take special note of verifiable facts such as dates and events. Highlight them and ask yourself if they are correct and decide if you need to provide more information or do any additional research. Here are some areas to look for:

❑ Dates
❑ Factual accuracy relating to events
❑ Spelling of names, especially of well-known people

- ❑ Spelling of place names
- ❑ Locations
- ❑ Correct usage of any diacritical marks (*'okina* or *kahakō*) and that they are used consistently throughout your manuscript (see below for more on Hawaiian diacritical marks)
- ❑ Quotes, poems, song lyrics, excerpts (Note: You may also need to obtain permission to use these.)
- ❑ Any math or timeframes ("From 1968 to 1978 we lived in Maui...they were the best eight years of our life.")
- ❑ If you reference websites, especially specific URLs, check the spellings and ensure the links are still live
- ❑ If you include recipes or instructions of any kind, make sure measurements or directions are correct

✳ **COPY EDITING:** You can do this as you go, but you'll want to be careful not to try to do too many things at the same time. This is often best saved for last, as the many revisions, additions and deletions may resolve grammar, tense, point of view and other similar issues. Things to consider at this final stage:

- ❑ *Grammar, tenses, subjects, verbs, punctuation, unnecessary repetition.* In particular, limit your use of exclamation points (in dialogue and in the narrative) and ellipses (those dot dot dots...) and make sure your commas or punctuation marks are properly tucked inside quotation marks for dialogue.
- ❑ *Spell checker, beware!* Watch for words that slip by spell checkers such as homonyms (words that sound the same but have different meanings such as "there," "their" and "they're"), compound words incorrectly divided (such as "bedroom," not "bed room") or words missing a letter (such as "tree" instead of "three").
- ❑ *Clear any clutter.* If you can say the same thing with fewer words, get rid of the excess.
- ❑ *Typographical errors.* Be sure not to rely too heavily on your word processing program's spell check or find/replace functions. They can unwittingly change words and phrases. Be sure to read each sentence carefully and to confirm any automatic changes.
- ❑ *Overall presentation and consistency.* If writing in chapters, is the presentation consistent?
- ❑ *The use of Hawaiian diacritical marks.* If your memoir includes Hawaiian words or phrases, consider using diacritical markings. Diacritical markings are marks placed over or attached to a letter to indicate proper pronunciation. The Hawaiian language has two diacritical marks: the 'okina, a glottal stop which indicates a break in the breath ("oh-oh"), and the kahakō, a macron which indicates an elongated vowel. The 'okina is an upside-down apostrophe that looks like the number six ('). Remember that the 'okina mark is not a straight (') or regular apostrophe (') and not an accent mark (`). The kahakō is a line placed directly above the vowel to be elongated. It's recommended that diacritical marks be used to properly reflect the correct spelling and usage of any Hawaiian words but many books still do not do so. It's up to you—many word processing programs have diacritical mark choices built in under "Fonts" or "Symbols."

HŌ‘IKE HO‘OPŌKOLE: CHAPTER SUMMARY

✓ Good writing involves revisions.

✓ Experienced writers know that editing is where the fun begins.

✓ A lot of the basic editing skills you'll need are already in your head.

✓ All writers need to know how to cast a careful eye over their manuscript.

✓ Approach your revisions with a plan.

✓ There are two kinds of editing: copy editing and content editing.

✓ Our goal is to make the memoir stronger, better, more readable, more compelling.

✓ If you need a short break between writing and editing, take it, but don't be gone for too long.

CHAPTER SEVEN
FEEDBACK AND SHARING

Kākoʻo

With an edited and revised manuscript in hand, it's time to get feedback from people you trust. This is an important part of the writing process, especially if you have plans to publish or publicly share your work. This round of feedback is designed to strengthen your work, to help you see things that you might otherwise miss.

OTHER WRITERS, OTHER READERS

You can call on trusted readers to give you feedback at any point in your writing process, but unless you have family or friends who are willing to look at your work-in-progress, save their reads until you have an edited manuscript. By the time you type the last line, you know exactly what's going on and have already made the initial decisions about what to keep in and what to exclude. Getting feedback too early in the process can slow things down, and you'll spend too much time reworking parts that you might end up changing or even deleting later.

> *"Have someone [you] trust, who has the skills of critical thinking and intelligence and knows enough about the author to offer meaningful comments and suggestions."*
> **BEN CAYETANO**

When choosing the best people to give you feedback on your manuscript, don't choose close family and friends just because they happen to be there. You want to choose people who are willing to read your work with a careful eye, who are open and understanding of the feedback you're looking for, who have an appreciation for words and how they appear on the page. Too often when we call on people close to us to give us feedback, it gets tangled with other things—our need for approval or for them to like our work. Their own feelings and emotions may get confused as well, especially if they are familiar with you or the events in your manuscript and have an opinion about what you've written. If you happen to have a family member who's also a writer, it can be even more challenging for them and for you. It's often difficult for people close to us to be objective, and when we put them on the spot to give us an objective review, we set them up to fail. Consider carefully whom you want to share this work with, and why. There will be plenty of time later for you to share your work in its final, carefully polished form.

Those close to us also have a way, sometimes inadvertently, of wounding us with their words. They're too close to us, and possibly even too close to our work. Find avid readers whom you believe would be drawn to memoirs like yours, and not just because they know you. Somebody who only reads romance novels or books on how to retile their bathroom may not be the best person to give you feedback on your memoir, especially if they don't read memoirs as a rule. A reader who lived through the same time, events or place or who has knowledge of the topic you are writing about can provide helpful editorial advice, but a true test of how well your manuscript holds up is if the uninitiated—but interested—reader understands it clearly. Choose your readers carefully and then be sure to tell them exactly what kind of feedback you're looking for.

HOʻĀʻO: TRY THIS

Feedback
When asking for feedback, be clear and purposeful about the kind of feedback you are looking for. Some questions you can ask:

* What did you like?
* What do you want more of?
* What do you want less of?
* How well did everything flow?
* What parts were confusing?
* Were you satisfied in the end?
* How did you feel when you finished reading?

Agree on a timeframe for them to get back to you with comments—don't let it be open-ended. Decide if you want to hear about typos and other nit-picky details. Those details do matter, but use your readers for top level feedback and let them know that you are aware that some grammatical errors may exist but that you plan on catching those later so they don't feel obligated to take out their red pen.

INFORMATION, NOT APPROVAL

Remember that everyone has different tastes, styles and preferences. Just because somebody gives you feedback doesn't mean they're right or that you have to make those changes. On the other hand, if someone's suggestion rubs you the wrong way, ask yourself why the comment bothers you before discounting it. Always listen with open ears, because sometimes those suggestions can make a good manuscript even better. Just don't always assume that because one person makes a suggestion you have to follow it.

"One person's purple is another person's periwinkle."
BETH-ANN KOZLOVICH

Be careful, too, not to be defensive about your work. It's hard not to, especially since the material is true and about you and your experience and feelings. But if you start to feel defensive, angry, misunderstood or disillusioned, you cloud your ability to make good choices about your book. Take a step back. Ask yourself again if the reader was chosen because of their ability to read your work objectively and with great interest, and not because you wanted them to love it and tell you you're awesome. Share your work with the primary purpose of getting helpful feedback that will strengthen your memoir. Information, not approval.

If you're feeling sensitive about sharing your work or don't have anyone you feel comfortable giving it to, skip ahead to the next chapter and then come back when you are ready. At some point, however, you'll need to let the work go and get it into the hands of early readers so you know what needs to be done before you share with a broader audience, even if your goal is to make the memoir available to only a small circle of people.

Oh, and one more thing: Don't forget to thank them for taking the time to read your manuscript!

WRITING GROUPS

If readers around you feel too close, another option is to join a writing group. Many communities throughout Hawai'i have writing groups that meet regularly. Check with the library and community centers to see if they know of any in your area. There are also online writing and feedback groups. You can also create a writing group of your own.

There are pros and cons to working with others on your manuscript. A definite pro is that you get feedback from several people at once. A con is that group feedback can be a mixed bag of helpful and unhelpful comments. Some people seem to relish the opportunity to be critical about another person's work. Others are reluctant to provide any truly helpful feedback at the risk of hurting your feelings.

"One of my most productive writing group sessions consisted of just my sister and my dad, neither of whom are writers, but both of whom are avid readers. After they both read a late draft of my book, we went to a bar, and they talked about the book as if they'd just gotten out of a movie theater. They didn't address me once—for two hours I was invisible. I just listened and took down notes."
MARK PANEK

You'll have to use your best judgment but remember that feedback can always be delivered in a spirit of kindness and encouragement. Even if it's clear you may have quite a bit of work ahead of you, you should feel better, not worse, about what you've done.

Once you receive feedback, be it written or oral, you'll want to give yourself a little time to let the feedback settle. Consider what they had to say, even if you're convinced it's wrong or you disagree. If you can, play a little—give their suggestions a shot and see if your memoir is stronger and more compelling, or weaker and more diluted, as a result. Many authors have found that "playing" sometimes leads to another outcome that's ten times better than what you had originally written or what was suggested.

Be open to hearing what people have to say without defending your work or arguing your point. If you have to explain it for people to understand, then that's a big clue that you haven't quite done your job. It's not about being right or wrong, or even if something is true or untrue. It's about necessity. Does your memoir need it? Is it better with or without it? If the comments are about the writing, read the passage in question aloud a few times and see if you can "hear" the issue. Remember, just because someone says there's something wrong with your work doesn't necessarily mean that they are right, but always give yourself a chance to run through the possibilities to see if anything they say can help may your memoir stronger.

HIRED HELP

If you don't have ready access to readers or prefer to work with a professional, you always have the option of hiring an editor to give you feedback. Freelance editors abound, but just like finding a good accountant, you'll want to ask around and get a referral. Make sure that you have an opportunity to talk with them, preferably by phone or in person, and have a clear understanding of what they'll do (and not do), the time frame and the associated cost. You should receive a written letter or document detailing their editorial comments and possibly a follow-up phone conversation to explain any confusing notes or to answer any questions.

> *"Everyone needs an editor."*
> **LEE CATALUNA**

Hiring outside help has its pros and cons, too. On the pro side, you have a professional looking at your work, ideally somebody who has worked on other memoirs, possibly with a publishing house. They do this sort of work for a living, and even if you don't agree with all their comments and suggestions, they're used to that, too. They know how to give feedback and can engage in a focused discussion about what works and what doesn't. On the con side, it can get expensive. And if your manuscript will require a lot of work to get it into publishable shape, you may be looking at another edit down the road. If you are watching your pocketbook, make sure that you pull in help later, rather than earlier, in the writing process. Some writers share their work too early and discover that they've blown their budget while they still have a long way to go.

Consider a trial—give a prospective editor the first chapter and ask for their feedback. You may have to pay for this work, but it will be worth it. Once you have a chance to review their feedback and have an experience of communicating with them, you'll know if they're a good fit—or not. You'll also get a sense of whether or not you should wait and do a few more self-revisions.

HŌʻIKE HOʻOPŌKOLE: CHAPTER SUMMARY

✓ Feedback is designed to strengthen your work, to help you see things that you might otherwise miss.

✓ Choose people who are willing to read your work with a careful eye, who are open and understanding of the feedback you're looking for, who have an appreciation for words and how they appear on the page. Those with an understanding of the time, place or topic can be particularly insightful.

✓ Share your work with the primary purpose of getting helpful feedback that will strengthen your memoir. Information, not approval.

✓ Give yourself a little time to let the feedback settle.

✓ Arriving at the best solution for any problems in your memoir is sometimes only possible after having experimented with a few possibilities.

✓ If hiring outside help, consider a trial period first.

CHAPTER EIGHT
RESTING

Ho'omaha

That's all we do here.

We rest.

We put the manuscript aside and turn our attention back to our lives. We give our writing, revisions and incorporated feedback a break from us as much as the other way around. We step back so our memoir has room to breathe.

How much time is enough time? It's up to you but somewhere in the range of more than a week but less than a year seems to work. You want to step far enough away so you forget about the way your story appears on the page, about whether or not you should add or remove anything else, about how clunky the whole thing might feel despite all your hard work. Let enough time pass so that the memoir becomes a little fuzzy, a memory in itself.

Think of this time as a good night's sleep, one in which you wake fully refreshed. Not groggy with your pillow over your head. Not exhausted and bleary-eyed. You wake ready for your day, eager for what's to come. When you feel this way about your memoir, it's time to get back to work.

Read through your memoir in its entirety, from start to finish. Just read—don't have a pen nearby, don't mark anything up. Resist the temptation to fix anything. Clear your throat a few times and read it aloud. When you get to the end of your memoir, decide if you're in need of a few more revisions or if you're ready to move to the next step: publication.

CHAPTER NINE
PUBLICATION

Pa'i

What are your hopes with your memoir? We say we write for ourselves and that is always the first step. But what about publication? In simplest terms, publication means to print or make your work available to others. In this digital age, publication can take on many forms, including print publication, online publication, digital book publication and/or audio publication. Print publication can be books or magazine articles. Books can be printed commercially (printed with a large or small publisher who shares in the sales of your books) or self-published (where you assume full responsibility for the production and distribution of your book). There are also hybrids that combine several of these forms. In other words, there are many options available to you.

WHY PUBLISH?

The recent boom in memoir writing and memoir reading is a result of a growing passion to hear the stories that make up our world. In some cases, memoirs serve to entertain, to lift us from our own lives and into the lives of others. In other cases, memoirs serve as reassurance—we are not alone, someone else has been where we are.

We publish our work when we want to share the stories of our life. People read in search of connection. That's what makes your story so valuable.

> *"The most rewarding part of publishing is that you have shared your story with an audience. Isn't that why we became writers in the first place—to share stories with the world?"*
> **PAMELA VARMA BROWN**

If you think you want to publish, we need to shift from the art of writing to the business of writing. Your first step is to determine who your audience is. Whom do you envision reading this book and how comfortable are you sharing your memoir, possibly with strangers? Are you interested in having only a few copies for friends and family, or are you hoping to see your memoir on bookstore shelves? What published memoirs are similar to yours or have similar themes?

It goes without saying that the higher your ambition, the more work you will have to put into perfecting your memoir and managing all the moving parts that come with getting your book out there. There are many resources to help you in your decision making and a simple search on the Internet will point you in the right direction. It's hard to know where to begin, however, so here are a few simple thoughts to get you started.

HOʻĀʻO: TRY THIS

A Publishing Questionnaire

Ask yourself a few simple questions to determine where you (and your manuscript) are in relation to publication:

* Who would enjoy reading (and spending money) on my memoir?

* Which published memoirs are similar to my mine?

* How do I feel about having family and close friends read my story?

* How do I feel about having strangers read my story?

* Am I telling my story or someone else's? If it's the latter, do I need to obtain any special permissions or consider rewriting any part of my memoir?

* How much time do I have available to devote to getting my memoir published?

* How much money do I have available to devote to getting my memoir published?

* Do I know any published authors who can help me on this journey?

* Am I willing to heavily revise or edit my memoir?

* Am I willing to educate myself on what it will take to get my memoir published?

* Am I easily discouraged?

* Am I willing to do (and have funds available to spend on) marketing on my own?

* Can I envision myself telling friends, family members, strangers, individuals and/or large groups about my memoir?

* Do I feel comfortable encouraging those people to purchase my book?

* Am I a part of any networks that can help me promote my memoir?

ENDORSEMENTS AND REVIEWS

Endorsements and reviews help sell books. They work in the same way as a friend saying, "Oh, you haven't read this yet? I read it straight through in one sitting, I couldn't put it down." Endorsements and reviews tell a potential reader, "We like this book. Buy it." As an author, you can't say that about your own book, and even if you did, nobody would listen. Glowing blurbs from an unknown author (or a family member) may be treated with skepticism. Readers prefer independent sources telling them that your book is worthy of their time.

Commercially published books usually have endorsements (also known as "blurbs") and reviews on the cover and/or inside the book. If you choose to self-publish, you'll still want to consider including these. For blurbs, contact well-known published authors, preferably ones with books similar to yours, whom readers may recognize. If you don't know any published authors, find ones you feel would be a good fit for your book and contact them any-way. Most authors have

> *"It is very helpful to have people endorse your book because it can open doors for you. New readers will get to know you because they trust the person endorsing you."*
> **LAURIE RUBIN**

websites and an email form that allows you to get in touch with them. You can also contact industry professionals for blurbs. If your memoir has an Alzheimer's component to it, consider getting in touch with national or local Alzheimer's organizations for a blurb. The worst thing anybody can say is no (or not respond), but in the off-chance they say yes, it will help your book tremendously.

If you have taken the time to make your memoir publishable, you should be able to find two to five reputable people to give your book the blurbs it deserves. Blurbs also help you sell your book to an agent or publisher—again, it's a bit like getting a letter of recommendation (in this case, in two or three sentences) and will help you stand out among the other submissions.

Reviews are different from endorsements or blurbs in that they speak specifi-cally to the work and the writing. You'll want to see if you can receive a review from newspapers, industry publications, national magazines, blogs, even televi-sion shows that routinely review new books. The larger and more prominent the publication, the more competitive it is to get their attention especially if you are a self-published author. Authors whose work is published through publishing houses usually have access to a marketing and publicity team that will help gather reviews but even then there is no guarantee of a review. Blurbs tend to remain firmly in the domain of the author whether published or self-published. In either case you, as the author, should do what you can to line up blurbs and reviews for your book even if you have a team of people helping you.

You'll need to gather blurbs and reviews prior to the final publication of your book. This means sending out manuscripts (once they've agreed to look at your memoir) or a printed copy of your book, bound by a copy center or with a binder clip. Some may agree to an electronic copy so make sure you know how to send your manuscript as an Adobe PDF (portable document format), which many prefer to a word processing document. Plan ahead with your requests as you should give potential blurbers the courtesy of three to five weeks to read your book. Reviewers may take up to two months and generally have guidelines you'll need to follow if you'd like them to consider your book.

COMMERCIAL PUBLISHING

Commercial publishing, or traditional publishing, refers to the way books have been published for decades. These publishers, both large and small, sign an agreement with an author to publish, or pay for the printing, of the book in exchange for a percentage of the sales. These publishers then help you prepare the book for publication and assume responsibility for both the publication and distribution of the book. They usually have the final say on cover design, artwork and edits even though they may ask for initial feedback from the author. In many cases they will also help with procuring reviews and marketing your book but this varies by publisher.

> *"Back in the day, I was whining to a college professor about how tough writing short stories and novels were. He smiled knowingly and said, 'If you think writing is tough, wait until you try selling the stuff.'"*
> **CEDRIC YAMANAKA**

Commercial publishers include large national and international companies (such as Penguin Random House, HarperCollins, Simon & Schuster) but also include academic presses (such as Kamehameha Publishing, University of

Hawai'i Press, East-West Center, Bishop Museum Press) and regional independent presses (such as Watermark Publishing, Mutual Publishing, Bess Press, Koa Books). A complete list of local publishers can be found via the Hawai'i Book Publishers Association (hawaiipublishers.org). These publishers have access to national distributors that can get your book into bookstores, both brick and mortar as well as online. This is one of the biggest advantages to going with a commercial publisher.

However, there's a catch to publishing your book commercially. In some cases you'll need a literary agent to represent you—smaller publishers are accustomed to working with authors directly but you can't approach large publishers without an agent. A literary agent generally takes a 15% commission for domestic sales and 20% for international sales. This may seem like a lot but remember that literary agents can help you not only find a publishing house for your memoir, but may sell other rights (foreign, film, audio, serial or magazine rights) to your work as well—not a simple task for a self-published author. Finding a literary agent can be daunting, as most agents have become as selective as publishing houses. You don't "hire" literary agents—they need to accept you as a client based on their love of your book and whether they see potential in the market for its success. Books listing literary agencies are updated annually and there are submission guidelines you'll need to follow in order to have your work read and considered.

Another challenge with commercially publishing your work is the length of time involved. Expect a year or two to find a literary agent, and up to another year for your agent to find a publishing house. Once you sign with a publishing house, it could be another twelve to eighteen months before your book hits the shelves. This protracted and sometimes discouraging process (which has to do in part with the very thorough editing and sales efforts) is why many new authors are turning to self-publication.

SELF-PUBLISHING

The dawn of digital publication has arrived, and with it a multitude of new ways to self-publish your memoir. Unlike the past when self-publication referred to vanity presses and was often stigmatized by poorly written work, these days many self-published authors are finding new ways of getting their work out there and finding success. Many high-quality self-published books have found space on bookshelves alongside their traditionally published counterparts.

> *"Find a way to get it printed...unlike a typed manuscript that gets tucked away in a drawer somewhere, a printed book sits on a shelf and waits for the family members to come along who are interested. And they will come along."*
> **LESLIE LANG**

Self-publication, or indie publication, basically refers to the production, printing and distribution of your book. But this can mean anything from printing copies on your printer to working with a reputable self-publishing company offering a full suite of professional publishing, design and marketing services. You can explore publishing your book solely on a digital platform through online bookstores or have books printed on demand, or both.

One of the greatest challenges to self-published authors is ensuring that their work is ready to be published. With you alone filling the roles of writer, editor, marketer and publisher, it's easy to cut corners in the interest of just getting it done. It looks good enough to you, after all, and you really can't see how another pass through your manuscript will make much of a difference.

Well, it can make a big difference. The disadvantage of wearing so many hats is that it's not only easy to get overwhelmed, it's easy to make mistakes. Your writer brain may remember a reference to Auntie Teani but a former edit may have removed that. So when her name appears later in your memoir without the previous reference, readers may get confused. But you don't catch this subtle error because your brain remembers everything, including previous drafts. You just assume it's in there, somewhere.

Another challenge for self-published authors is avoiding the "self-published look." This means poor artwork and formatting. "If you are self-publishing, you absolutely need professional editing and a professionally designed book cover," Leslie Lang says. You can either hire these experts individually or go with a company that provides self-publishing services. These can include everything from editorial help to marketing and distribution, all under one roof. For the self-published author, publication options abound.

Regardless of what you decide to do, remember that you will need to be diligent in understanding all of the pieces that need to come together before your book hits the shelves, digitally or otherwise. Take the time to educate yourself on what it means to self-publish and listen to the stories of those who have walked the path before you. After all of your hard work in crafting your memoir, don't let up now.

BOOK FORMATS

When we say "book," what do we mean? It can be a printed book, either hardcover or softcover (paperback), it can be digital (there are several different types of e-book formats) or it can be audio. All three of these options are available to you as a self-published or traditionally published author.

"People often say, 'I want to leave a story for my children or grandchildren,' but if you push a bit, they'll also say, 'And I want a big trade publisher and a national book tour.' If the story really is for your family, that's great—but then you don't need a publisher, because there are so many self-publishing options available that allow you to leave your relatives exactly what you want, without the necessary revisions and compromises that go along with professional publishing."
CRAIG HOWES

The printed form is what many of us grew up with. We browse libraries and bookstores by pulling titles off a shelf and reading the back cover or flipping through the book. If you work with a traditional publisher, it is usually for a physical book (though they almost always include a digital format as well). If you self-publish, gone are the days where you would have to house an inventory of 5,000 books in your garage. The publishing industry has changed so that single and small print runs are simple and not cost-prohibitive for traditional and self-publishers alike.

The fastest format is the digital form. Many self-published authors opt for this choice because it's quicker than the printed route. Once your book is ready (having been edited to perfection or near-perfection), you can upload it and have it available for sale within a matter of days. Updates and changes are easy, too, and self-published authors like that they can change the price of their e-book or offer promotional pricing whenever they want. The most common digital formats are ePub (which can be read on your computer and across several platforms such as digital readers, phones, iPads, etc.), .AZW or .MOBI (for Amazon's proprietary Kindle reader) and PDF (which can be read using Adobe Acrobat or Adobe Reader). Many word-processing programs can convert documents to these formats, or a self-publishing service can convert the files for you to be read on different devices.

The audiobook form is a good option for readers who like to read on the go—in their car or on the plane, even while they're running or on a stationary bike. You can work through companies like Audible which helps authors self-produce audiobooks if they have a digital and physical book already for sale.

The bottom line is this: Once you have a finished manuscript, you have choices. You can decide *who* you want to publish your book (a traditional publisher, you, or a hybrid of the two in the form of a self-publishing company that assists in the production aspect of your book) and then *how* you want to publish your book (print, digital, audio). It's exciting to know that, one way or another, readers might soon be able to enjoy your story.

A FINAL, GENTLE REMINDER

Whatever you end up doing, remember the reason you embarked on this journey to begin with. The goal has been, and continues to be, you telling your story. That is what really matters. That you took the time to look back on your life and write down what feels important, what's worth remembering—that is what this process is all about.

> *"People are their stories."*
> **BETH-ANN KOZLOVICH**

Remember that the most important work has already happened.

You are a writer. And you have told your story.

For now, we are *pau.*

HŌʻIKE HOʻOPŌKOLE: CHAPTER SUMMARY

✓ Write for yourself first.

✓ Know your audience.

✓ The higher your ambition, the more you need to be prepared for the amount of work that comes with readying your memoir for publication.

✓ Endorsements and reviews help inform readers and sell your book.

✓ There are many options available to authors these days: commercial publishing, self-publishing, or a combination of the two.

✓ Books can exist in any or all of these forms: print (in hardcover or softcover), digital (e-book) or audio.

✓ Whatever you choose to do, the most important work has been done: You are a writer, and you have told your story.

WHAT'S NEXT

Heaha Hou A'e

The next story.
The next book.
The next horizon.
Let this be the beginning, and dive back in.
Hana hou.

APPENDIX A
WRITING A PERSONAL ESSAY

Personal essays are short pieces of writing that address a given topic from a writer's own perspective. Subject matters include contemporary situations or the author's opinion about a political, social or ethical dilemma. It's considered a form of expository writing which generally serves to inform, instruct and/or explain a process. It's grounded in fact rather than reflection or emotions, even though the writer may include examples from their life to illustrate a point. Articles, letters, reports and academic papers are all examples of expository writing. Consider the personal essay the analytical brother on the family tree of life-writing.

Writing the personal essay is a great way to sharpen your writing skills and many publications (like magazines or newspapers) prefer the personal essay form to memoir because well-written personal essays effortlessly guide the reader to the desired conclusion. Writing a personal essay will train you as a writer to look closely at the experiences of your life and correlate them to a greater life theme or principle. You'll also learn to communicate an idea succinctly and purposefully.

Here are the key parts of a personal essay:

Introduction. Begin with a compelling statement about what your essay will be about. This is also known as the "hook" as it pulls the reader in. It also prepares the reader for what's to come. You'll want to make it clear as to why you are writing this essay, how you were involved or what made the event important or memorable.

Body. This is where you write and offer facts to illustrate the point you are trying to make. Talk about what happened and provide any dramatic or pivotal moments. Be generous with details and give people a sense of time and place so they can anchor when and where things happened.

Conclusion. End with the moral of the story, the lesson or point you are trying to make. This would also be the place where you might offer some reflection or analysis of the experience. Follow the three R's: reiterate, review and reflect. Close with a powerful last thought or statement.

Personal essays are about brevity and usually range from 500 to 2,500 words. Different publications have different guidelines so be sure to review these carefully if you plan to submit your work. Some of the most successful personal essays are under 1,000 words, so if you are writing for yourself or plan to share your personal essay with family or friends, consider using 1,000 words as a guideline.

APPENDIX B
WRITING AN AUTOBIOGRAPHY

An autobiography is a factual account of your life, written by you. It starts with birth and generally continues through to the present day. Unlike the memoir, which is reflective and subjective in nature, the autobiography is grounded in fact and follows a chronological order of events. Many of the details are verifiable and/or irrefutable, such as your name, place of birth, parents, current residence, siblings and so on.

The idea of an autobiography is that it encompasses an entire life lived, at least until the point it was written. There's no skipping around or omissions—the autobiography is designed to provide a historical record of your life. While there may be reflection and aspects of an emotional journey, an autobiography tends to focus on information rather than recollection or memory.

Another way to look at the autobiography is to consider it a narrative résumé. Because the autobiography is comprehensive, people will usually write only one autobiography, generally when they are much older. A memoir, on the other hand, is a snapshot in time. A person may have one autobiography but can write several memoirs, each focusing on a different aspect of their life or time or place.

APPENDIX C
WRITING A BIOGRAPHY

A biography is a factual account of a life, written by someone other than the person serving as the subject. Like the autobiography, a biography tends to be presented in chronological order, starting with birth and generally continuing through to the present day or death. Biographies may also start with a pivotal or controversial moment and then flashback to the beginning.

Because biographies are written by other people, it is not unusual to have more than one biography written about someone, especially if the person is a celebrity or of political or historical importance. Biographies are grounded in fact, but may include a premise or assumption that the writer attempts to support by providing the relevant evidence. If factual data is in question, different writers may be writing to prove or disprove that data. Biographies usually include extensive interviews with family members, friends, coworkers or anyone who has a relationship or knowledge of the subject.

When writing a biography, begin by outlining your project. A clear table of contents will guide not only you but can assist in securing interviews if people have an idea about the scope of your project. Be sure to always answer the question *why* as well—why are you writing this biography? What inspired you, why do you feel it's important? Of all the people you could write about, why did you choose this person? How are you qualified—are you personally connected to this subject or subject matter? Knowing these answers will help you convey your enthusiasm for the project and keep you motivated during the writing.

Chris Vandercook offers this thought to help you guide your writing: "How would you want your own life portrayed? You'd want credit given where it's due, delivered with relevant detail—and you'd want its impact clearly understood. That's easy enough to understand. We all want our lives to mean something, and each of our lives has lessons to impart—if a writer can be found to do it justice."

You'll also want to be diligent in your fact checking and consider legal counsel for any sticky or complicated matters. Writing about other people's lives, whether dead or living, requires careful consideration but can also be a great service when written with the purpose of sharing inspirational, informative or entertaining stories that help inform our own lives. Again, the heart of any life story is the human connection. Find it in your writing and readers will respond.

APPENDIX D
WRITING A FAMILY HISTORY PROJECT

Family histories are a great way to capture a lot of genealogical information in one place and pass it down to future generations. They're particularly valuable because they can include interviews, photos, recipes and stories of multiple family members. Family histories are an opportunity to be creative and can include everyone from the oldest living relative to the youngest. Your biggest challenge will be determining the scope of your project so it's not too overwhelming.

Here are some questions to ask yourself when writing the family history:

* Is this a project that other members of my family support?
* Can I count on other family members to provide information?
* Who will be responsible for writing and compiling the information?
* Who will be responsible for any research, writing, editing or publication costs?
* What documents or personal records will be available to me?
* Do I need any special permissions (for example, to reprint letters, photos or newspaper articles in which family members may appear)?
* How do I envision my family history project when it's finished?
    - Who will be included?
    - How far back will it go?
    - Will it be a narrative, scrapbook, photo book, cookbook?
    - What is my time frame for researching, writing and publishing this book?
    - What do I plan to do with the book once it's finished?
* Is everyone in agreement that the book will (or will not) be made publicly available?
* Am I the author of the book, or will it be written by all of us?
* What will I do if someone says they don't want their story or details to be included?

In writing the family history, you must also decide how much detail to include. If there are skeletons in the family closet, are you going to mention them? If someone went to jail or has an embarrassing or humiliating experience, are you going to include it? As with all life stories, remember to always ask yourself *why* you are writing this book and *why* a particular story may be necessary or unnecessary. You will have to make decisions along the way lest you end up with a large tome nobody wants to read. Family histories are part posterity, part pleasure. It should be enjoyable to have a book like this in your home! It should inform and educate, yes, but it should be something everyone is proud of and eager to share. *This is you, this is where you came from, these are the people that make up your family.* Even if everyone agrees to collaborate on the project there will need to be one main person pulling to all together. Since you're the one reading this book, that person will most likely be you.

Organization is key for any family history project. Communicating what you need from the people involved will help everyone understand their contribution and keep the project moving forward.

APPENDIX E
WRITING CORPORATE AND ORGANIZATIONAL BIOGRAPHIES

Storytelling is a great way for businesses and organizations to build their brand and let their customers know who they really are. People connect with people, so sharing the history behind your organization gives others a chance to know the people they are doing business with.

In many ways a business or nonprofit is a living, breathing entity—it almost always takes on a life of its own beyond what the original founders may have intended. There's the birth of an idea, the growing pains, the ups and downs, the challenges, the successes. There may be people who've left an indelible mark, whose vision formed the organization and made it what it is today. Corporate and organizational biographies differ from executive biographies in that they are the story of the company itself—not just the story of an individual person.

Writing a corporate or organizational biography naturally includes the pertinent details of who, what, where, when and why, but there is also the opportunity to share the stories that make the business or organization unique. You can use it to establish expertise and credibility as well as connection and camaraderie. We all know the stories behind the big brands—Starbucks, Apple, McDonald's, WalMart. In Hawai'i, there's C.S. Wo & Sons, L&L Hawaiian Barbecue, Ben Franklin Crafts. Whether you are conscious of it or not, stories help businesses succeed.

Think of your organization's biography as an expanded About Us section from your website. This is a document that helps people decide if they want to engage. It is every bit as personal as choosing whom you want to be friends with.

You can keep it simple. Start with these pieces of information and grow from there:

* What is the story you really want to tell? What do you want people to know about your business or organization?
* What was the year and location of the organization's founding? The names of the people who founded it?
* Why was the organization founded?
* Are there any interesting stories about what happened in the beginning?
* Describe the first location, building or office.
* If possible, interview the founders or their descendants and get their reflections and memories.
* Write about the early years. Who were the customers or clients?
* Write about key people in the organization. What did they do and how did it affect or change the organization?

* Include mission statements, governing values, financials, notable clients or customers, important deals or partnerships, organization name changes, mergers, acquisitions, multiple locations, growth and hardships.
* Include visuals such as logos, photographs, original documentation, letters, name badges, newspaper announcements and so on.
* Include any profiles of the organization that appeared in magazines, newspapers or books.
* Include the board of directors, staff and other key members or partners.
* End with a look towards the future. What's next?
* Sometimes the best stories come from the people in the trenches. Find those who have been there the longest and ask them to reflect on how the organization has changed (or not).

Corporate and organizational biographies will most likely be reviewed by the organization's legal counsel. Be sure to secure any necessary permissions. The focus of a corporate or organizational biography is on the facts, but sharing the stories, hopes and dreams of the people involved will make it something people will want to read.

APPENDIX F
TAKING ORAL HISTORY

In Hawai'i, oral history plays an important role. Stories are gathered, told and passed on in this way, from one person to another. In some cases, it is the only way in which history, customs or beliefs are passed on. Many old timers eschew the use of audio or video recorders, even pencil and paper. Often times the story they tell is for your ears only, selected just for you because they know it is something you need to hear.

The best oral historians are storytellers. When someone tells you a story, it is important that you listen with your whole being. Try not to be sidetracked with note taking or fiddling with a recorder, even if they give you permission to record the meeting. Hopefully they will, because many of these stories have great value.

There are two approaches when it comes to oral history. One is to let the person talk and gently guide the conversation. The other is to establish more of a question-and-answer scenario, one in which you have specific questions prepared in advance. In both cases you will want to sharpen your listening skills.

"Your biggest challenge will likely be to stay out of the way," says Mark Panek. "Your job is to listen and listen." It's okay to occasionally ask a question or push for more details. If you are interviewing them, be sure to record the interview and transcribe the notes yourself. Panek also recommends showing them the pages in which they may appear. "Nothing you write will ever come out the way your interviewees think it will."

Author Billy Bergin agrees. "Let them read your work when done, as further interviews will be welcomed by them with trust of your integrity." He recommends a strong dose of humility on your part while extending dignity to whomever is being interviewed. In preparing for his interviews, Bergin will research and mention significant contributions a person may have made but "were never reported often due to the humble nature of many people." As embarrassed as your subjects may be, they may also appreciate the time you took to acknowledge what they've done. And, in true Hawaiian style, Bergin suggests bringing a small gift. "Take a token—flowers, sweets, beer—or whatever you know they would appreciate."

Gail Miyasaki also believes that doing research prior to the meeting will arm you with a basic understanding of the history surrounding the person or event. "You may need to pull from the larger design of history to encourage recollections of the personal story that occurred against that backdrop," she says. Ask for details and feelings, and do so gently. "Persist with women," she adds. For many older-generation minority women, there may be a reluctance or discomfort in sharing their stories. "Ask a sister or good friend to sit in to raise the comfort level."

Pamela Varma Brown advises that you let the conversation flow as if you were talking to a friend, being open to where the conversation may lead. "The more you enjoy what your interviewee is talking about," she says, "the more they will want to share with you."

Warren Nishimoto, Director for the Center for Oral History, University of Hawai'i at Mānoa, offers this checklist of reminders when gathering oral history. Preparation is key and can ensure that time spent with whomever are you interviewing is efficient and enjoyable for both of you.

HOW TO GATHER ORAL HISTORY

❑ Pre-plan your interviews
❑ Establish a question-and-answer format
❑ Focus on subjects of historical interest
❑ Select a willing interviewee who is physically and mentally able
❑ Be a prepared, knowledgeable interviewer
❑ Remember to listen: Ninety-five percent of effective oral history interviewing is the ability to listen to what's being said
❑ Remember to establish rapport: The trust you build with your interviewee is critical to the success of any interviewing project

APPENDIX G
RESOURCES

Here are some additional books on writing memoir:

Courage and Craft: Writing Your Life into Story by Barbara Abercrombie

Writing & Selling Your Memoir: How to Craft Your Life Story So That Somebody Else Will Actually Want to Read It by Paula Balzer

Writing the Memoir: From Truth to Art by Judith Barrington

Writing a Life: Teaching Memoir to Sharpen Insight, Shape Meaning—and Triumph Over Tests by Katherine Bomer

Memoir: An Introduction by G. Thomas Couser

Writing as a Way of Healing: How Telling Our Stories Transforms Our Lives by Louise DeSalvo

Writing Your Life: An Easy-to-Follow Guide to Writing an Autobiography by Mary Borg and Joyce Mihran Turley

Old Friend from Far Away: The Practice of Writing Memoir by Natalie Goldberg

The Situation and the Story: The Art of Personal Narrative by Vivian Gornick

You Can't Make This Stuff Up: The Complete Guide to Writing Creative Nonfiction—from Memoir to Literary Journalism and Everything in Between by Lee Gutkind

Will Write for Food: The Complete Guide to Writing Cookbooks, Restaurant Reviews, Articles, Memoir, Fiction and More by Dianne Jacob

Handling the Truth: On the Writing of the Memoir by Beth Kephart

Turning Memories Into Memoirs: A Handbook for Writing Lifestories by Denis Ledoux

The Heart and Craft of Lifestory Writing: How to Transform Memories Into Meaningful Stories by Sharon M. Lippincott

The Art of the Personal Essay: An Anthology from the Classical Era to the Present by Philip Lopate

Shimmering Images: A Handy Little Guide to Writing Memoir by Lisa Dale Norton

So You Want to Write: How to Master the Craft of Writing Fiction and Memoir by Marge Piercy and Ira Wood

Writing Life Stories: How To Make Memories Into Memoirs, Ideas Into Essays And Life Into Literature by Bill Roorbach

Legacy: A Step-By-Step Guide to Writing Personal History by Linda Spence

Thinking About Memoir by Abigail Thomas

The Autobiographer's Handbook: The 826 National Guide to Writing Your Memoir by Jennifer Traig

Memoir: A History by Ben Yagoda

Inventing the Truth: The Art and Craft of Memoir by William Zinsser

And a few other books that I've found very helpful:

Wired for Story: The Writer's Guide to Using Brain Science to Hook Readers From the Very First Sentence by Lisa Cron

The Writer's Legal Guide by Tad Crawford and Kay Murray

The Storytelling Animal: How Stories Make Us Human by Jonathan Gottschall

On Writing: A Memoir of the Craft by Stephen King

Bird by Bird: Some Instructions on Writing and Life by Anne Lamott

The Forest for the Trees: An Editor's Advice to Writers by Betsy Lerner

If You Want to Write: A Book About Art, Independence and Spirit by Brenda Ueland

The Writer's Journey: Mythic Structure for Writers by Christopher Vogler

ABOUT THE EXPERTS

Billy Bergin was born and raised on the Big Island of Hawai'i. He attended Kansas State University, where he received a doctorate in veterinary medicine in 1967 then went on to establish the first private large animal veterinary practice on the Big Island. He served as chief veterinarian at Parker Ranch from 1970 to 1995. Since 1971 Billy has been a medical officer with the Livestock and Disease Control Division, State of Hawai'i Department of Agriculture. He is the author of the *Loyal to the Land: The Legendary Parker Ranch* series.

Pamela Varma Brown (kauaistories.net) is the publisher and editor of the book *Kauai Stories,* a collection of inspiring, humorous and touching personal stories about life on the Garden Island of Kaua'i. Pam's passion is bringing people's stories to light, both in written form and by talking story in person. She has lived on Kaua'i since 1988.

Bob Buss has been executive director of the Hawai'i Council for the Humanities, an affiliate of the National Endowment for the Humanities, since 2004 after having served as program officer for twenty years. Bob works with local community and cultural centers, museums, archives, schools and libraries to facilitate public humanities programs, and was the founding coordinator for Hawai'i History Day in 1990. His academic interests include Confucianism and Buddhism, ethics and philosophy of art.

Lee Cataluna has her M.F.A. in creative writing from the University of California, Riverside. She worked as a journalist in Hawai'i for twenty years. Her plays have been seen in theaters across the state, and her books have been published by Bamboo Ridge. She teaches creative writing at 'Iolani School.

Benjamin J. Cayetano served as governor of Hawai'i from 1994 to 2002 and was the first Filipino-American elected as a United States governor. His memoir, *BEN: A Memoir from Street Kid to Governor,* was published in 2009. He currently lives in Honolulu with his wife, Vicky.

Stuart Holmes Coleman (stuart-coleman.com) is a freelance writer and award-winning author of *Eddie Would Go* and *Fierce Heart.* Coleman has been awarded the Elliot Cades Award for Literature, the Hawai'i Book Publisher Association's Excellence in Non-Fiction Award and the Yemassee Award for Best Poetry along with fellowships to the Mesa Refuge and the Norman Mailer Writers Colony. He currently works as the Hawai'i coordinator of the Surfrider Foundation.

Craig Howes has been director of the Center for Biographical Research since 1997. He has served as an editor of *Biography: An Interdisciplinary Quarterly* since 1994 and as an instructor of English at the University of Hawai'i at Mānoa since 1980. The Principal Scholar of the television documentary series *Biography Hawai'i,* he also co-edited *Teaching Life Writing Texts* (MLA, 2008) with Miriam Fuchs. His book, *Voices of the Vietnam POWs,* was a *Choice* magazine notable academic selection.

Patricia Jennings was born in Hāmākua on the Big Island, grew up on various sugar plantations, married at an early age and lived in St. Louis for seventeen years, had five children, moved back to Hawai'i, was widowed and then married an Australian, living in the bush for almost twenty years before returning to Hawai'i. Her memoir, *Georgia O'Keefe's Hawai'i*, was published in 2011.

Frances Kakugawa (francesk.org) is an award-winning author of poetry, children's books and memoirs. A former educator, she travels throughout the U.S. giving lectures and workshops on caregiving, poetry and writing. She resides in Sacramento where she conducts poetry support groups for caregivers and memoir and general poetry writing sessions. Frances is a former resident of the Big Island, born and raised in Kapoho.

Victoria Nalani Kneubuhl (hawaiimystery.com) is a Honolulu writer. Her plays have been performed in Hawai'i, the continental United States and have toured to Britain, Asia and the Pacific. She is the author of two mystery novels set in Hawai'i, *Murder Casts a Shadow* and *Murder Leaves Its Mark*. She is the writer and co-producer of the television series *Biography Hawai'i*. She has received the Hawai'i Award for Literature and the Elliot Cades Award for Literature.

Beth-Ann Kozlovich is Hawai'i Public Radio's Talk Shows executive producer and oversees HPR's five locally produced talk shows. In 1999, she created and began moderating "Town Square," HPR's long-running live public affairs forum. She created and co-hosts HPR2's weekday morning show, "The Conversation," launched in 2011. She was also the Hawai'i anchor of NPR's "Morning Edition."

Leslie Lang (leslielang.com) is a Big Island writer and editor. Her company, Talk Story Press, helps people create memoirs and family history books. Leslie wrote *Exploring Historic Hilo*, co-authored *Mauna Kea: A Guide to Hawai'i's Sacred Mountain* and has written hundreds of newspaper and magazine articles as well as worked for corporate and private clients. She also edits books for self-published authors. She is a member of the American Society of Journalists and Authors and of the Association of Personal Historians.

Gail Miyasaki is a freelance writer/editor in Honolulu. Her articles have appeared in *Hawaii Business*, HONOLULU, *Honolulu Family* and MANA magazines, among other publications. In the 1970s, she wrote extensively on the Japanese-American experience in Hawai'i as a staff writer for the *Hawai'i Herald*. She is the editor of *Japanese Eyes, American Heart, Volume II: Voices from the Home Front in World War II Hawai'i*.

Warren Nishimoto (oralhistory.hawaii.edu) is director of the Center for Oral History, University of Hawai'i at Mānoa. He has coordinated oral history projects documenting various aspects of the social, cultural and political history of Hawai'i. He serves as consultant to community-based oral history projects, publishes books and articles on oral history and Hawai'i's multicultural history, teaches classes at the university and to community members and speaks to community groups. Warren holds a Ph.D. in education from the University of Hawai'i at Mānoa.

Mark Panek is the author of *Hawai'i: A Novel*, written in the style of Tom Wolfe's researched-and-detailed new-journalistic realism. His first book, *Gaijin Yokozuna: A Biography of Chad Rowan*, was nominated for the *Los Angeles Times* Biography of the Year. His second, *Big Happiness: The Life and Death of a Modern Hawaiian Warrior*, won the Hawai'i Book Publisher's Association award for Excellence in Non-Fiction. A University of Hawai'i professor of creative writing, Mark was also recently honored with the Elliot Cades Award for Literature.

Laurie Rubin (laurie-rubin.com) is a mezzo-soprano who has been blind since birth. Praised by the *New York Times* for "her compelling artistry" and "communicative power," Laurie's career highlights include solo recital debuts at Wigmore Hall and Carnegie Hall. She is co-founder and associate artistic director of 'Ohana Arts, a performing arts school and festival in Hawai'i. She also designs her own line of handmade jewelry, LR Look. Her memoir, *Do You Dream in Color? Insights from a Girl Without Sight,* was published in 2012.

Phil Slott (philslott.com) has lived on the Big Island since 1989. A near-fatal crash with a drunk driver in 1993 inspired his forthcoming memoir, *Damage Control: A Brain Injury Survivor Helps You Beat the Odds.* Before moving to Hawai'i, Phil had a successful twenty-six year career in advertising as senior creative director and chairman of BBDO London. His best-known lines are "It's Not Just a Job, It's an Adventure" for the U.S. Navy and "Never Let 'em See You Sweat" for Gillette.

Christine Thomas (literarylotus.com) is a Honolulu-based writer focused on travel, culture, features and literary criticism. She is the editor of *Don't Look Back: Hawaiian Myths Made New*, a collection of Hawaiian legends retold for a modern audience, and her short fiction has been published in anthologies and literary magazines in the U.K. and U.S. She has taught creative writing and literature at Punahou School and to undergraduates across the country.

David Ulrich (creativeguide.com) is the program coordinator for Pacific New Media, University of Hawai'i at Mānoa. He is an active photographer and writer whose work has been widely published and exhibited. He is the author of *The Widening Stream: The Seven Stages of Creativity* and currently working on a memoir/essay: *Longing for Light: Into the Heart of Vision*. He is a consulting editor for *Parabola* magazine and a frequent contributor.

Chris Vandercook is a writer and musician who has worked as a television news producer and photographer, a political speechwriter and a program host on Hawai'i Public Radio. He was born in New York City and came to Hawai'i in 1983. He lives in Kailua and performs regularly as a jazz and blues guitarist.

Cedric Yamanaka is the author of *In Good Company*, a collection of short stories. He received the Helen Deutsch Fellowship from Boston University while completing his M.A. in creative writing. His fiction has been published in a number of literary journals. He lives in Honolulu.

ACKNOWLEDGMENTS

In Hawaiian, 'ohana means family. Not just those who are related to us by blood, but people we've chosen to connect with, people we've invited to be a part of our lives or who have invited us to be a part of theirs. This book has its own 'ohana, and those are the people I'd like to take a moment to thank.

A big mahalo to Dawn Sakamoto and George Engebretson at Watermark Publishing. They were, and continue to be, supportive creative partners.

There were those who took time from their busy schedules to connect with me about writing and sharing life stories. I've learned from all of them: Billy Bergin, Pamela Varma Brown, Bob Buss, Lee Cataluna, Ben Cayetano, Stuart Holmes Coleman, Craig Howes, Patricia Jennings, Frances Kakugawa, Victoria Nalani Kneubuhl, Beth-Ann Kozlovich, Leslie Lang, Gail Miyasaki, Warren Nishimoto, Mark Panek, Laurie Rubin, Phil Slott, Christine Thomas, David Ulrich, Chris Vandercook and Cedric Yamanaka. We are lucky to have them available to us as experts and resources. The following students, both young and old, made their six-word memoirs available to the world: Christian Gomez, Levi Higa, Ryan Hooley, Kai Ibana, George Manu, Elsbeth McKeen, Arielle Faith Michael, Kamuela Spencer-Herring and Taran Takahashi. Pamela Young offered the Foreword and shared her own story about the value of memoir. Danny Akaka Jr., director of cultural affairs at Mauna Lani Bay Hotel & Bungalows, not only took the time to meet with me and share his mana'o about Hawai'i's long history of oral tradition, but also blessed this book, my family's home, our children and our marriage over the years.

My gratitude to those who spend a good chunk of their life in my company: my husband, Darrin, and our three children, Maya, Eric and Luke. Our children were born here, two at North Hawai'i Community Hospital and one at home. I believe it's a privilege to have a childhood in Hawai'i; we are *all* lucky to live Hawai'i. Mahalo to my parents, Dr. I-Chi Hsu and my mother, Priscilla Liang Hsu. My mother came to Hawai'i in 1961 on a full scholarship from the East-West Center at UH Mānoa where she received her master's in social work. In many ways she was the first to walk the path we later got to follow.

In my upcountry cow town of Waimea (Kamuela), thanks to *North Hawaii News* editor Lisa Dahm, Waimea Community Education Director Matilda Tompson, Emily Hoover and Lisa O'Leary at Bentleys Home Collection. Janet Lam at North Kohala Library read a draft and offered valuable feedback. Leesa Robertson, English teacher at Waimea Middle School, shared her students with me. My memoir students and private writing clients were willing guinea pigs over the years for much of the content in this book—*mahalo nui loa*.

And to Stephene Bengene Lindsey, aka Aunty Tūtū, who embodies aloha and the pride, intelligence, talent and wisdom of her ancestors; it is to her that this book is dedicated.

DOWNLOAD WORKSHEETS,
FLASH CARDS & MORE FROM

WRITING THE HAWAI'I MEMOIR
Advice and Exercises to Help You Tell Your Story

Visit www.legacyislepublishing.net/memoir-guide
to download helpful worksheets, inspirational quote cards and
exercise flash cards.

**Remember, if you're writing, you're a writer.
Get started today!**

INDEX OF EXERCISES

Following is a list of *Ho'ā'o: Try This* exercises that appear in this book.

INDEX

ABOUT THE AUTHOR

Darien Gee is the nationally bestselling author of six novels, three written under the pen name Mia King. Her books have been translated into fourteen languages and are selections of the Doubleday, Literary Guild, Rhapsody and Book of the Month Club book clubs. Darien writes about writing and creativity in her column, "Writer's Corner," which appears weekly in *North Hawaii News*. She lives with her family in upcountry Hawai'i and is either corralling stories or kids while trying to figure out what to make for dinner. To learn more, please visit dariengee.com.

HOW WILL YOU TELL
Your STORY?

CREATE A LASTING LEGACY
FOR YOUR FAMILY OR BUSINESS

Legacy Isle Publishing is devoted to "Telling Hawai'i's Stories"—memoirs, family histories, corporate biographies and class projects—books and e-books created to share personal stories with aloha. With four customizable packages, we're here to help you preserve your *mo'olelo* for future generations, or to share your expertise and business legacy with your clients.

We are a division of **Watermark Publishing**, an Island publisher with more than two decades of experience in producing top-quality, award-winning books by and about Hawai'i's biggest names—Barack Obama, Don Ho, Ben Cayetano, "Gentleman Ed" Francis and others.

Legacy Isle Publishing accepts authors of adult nonfiction or children's books seeking to publish a product of truly professional quality. Our services include copyediting, design and production, proofreading and printing, and even a distribution option.

Select your package and start the publishing process at
www.legacyislepublishing.net

Need a fully customized quote?
Contact us at info@legacyislepublishing.

f facebook.com/LegacyIsle | @LegacyIsle